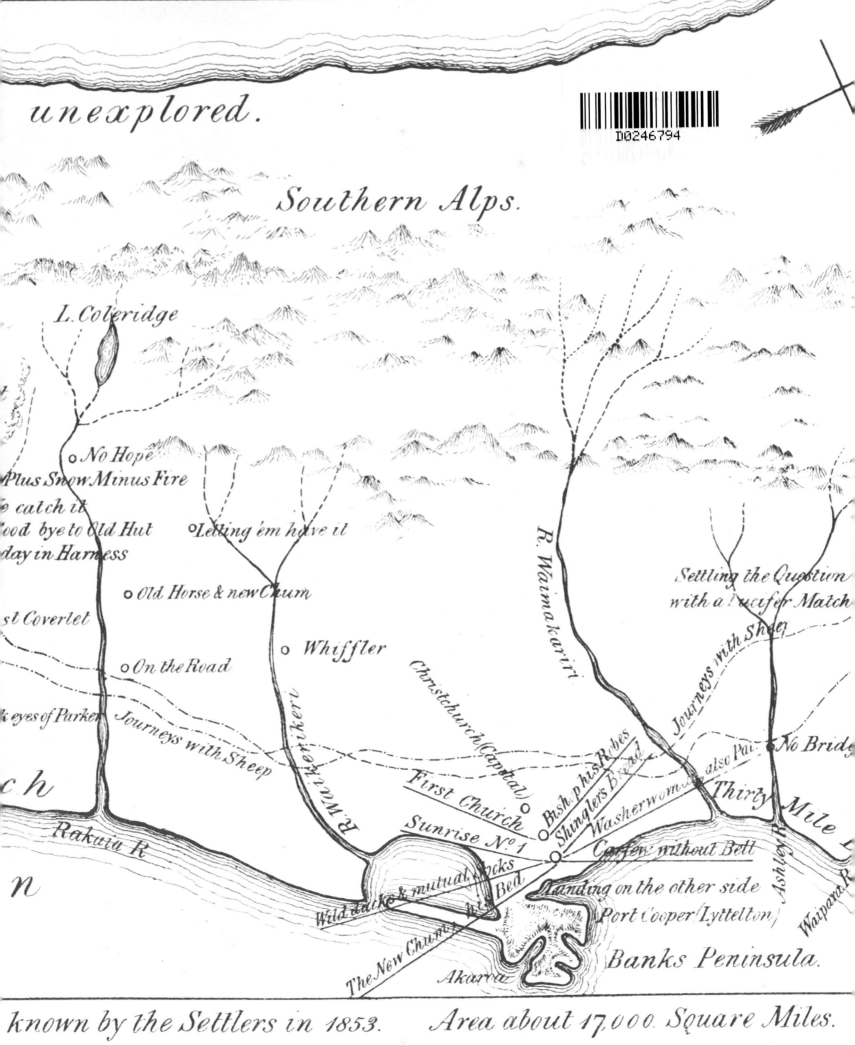

unexplored.

Southern Alps.

L. Coleridge

○ No Hope

Plus Snow Minus Fire

e catch it

ood bye to Old Hut

day in Harness

○ Letting 'em have it

○ Old Horse & new Chum

st Coverlet

○ Whiffler

○ On the Road

eyes of Parker

Journeys with Sheep

Settling the Question
with a Lucifer Match

Journeys with Sheep

R. Waimakariri

Christchurch (Capital)

R. Wainakariri

Bish: his Robes

Shingler's Bread

Washerwoman also Pai

No Bridg

Thirty Mile

First Church

Sunrise Nº 1

Curfew without Bell

ch

Rakaia R.

Wild ducks & mutual ocks Bed

Landing on the other side
Port Cooper (Lyttelton)

n

The New Chum

Akaroa

Banks Peninsula.

Ashley

Waipara R

known by the Settlers in 1853.   Area about 17,000 Square Miles.

st Longitude, & 43 South Latitude.

PRESENTING
NEW ZEALAND

PRESENTING
NEW ZEALAND

A Nation's Heritage

PHILIP TEMPLE

NH
NEW
HOLLAND

First published in 2001 by New Holland Publishers (NZ) Ltd
Auckland • Sydney • London • Cape Town

www.newhollandpublishers.com

218 Lake Road, Northcote, Auckland, New Zealand
14 Aquatic Drive, Frenchs Forest, NSW 2086, Australia
86 Edgware Road, London W2 2EA, United Kingdom
80 McKenzie Street, Cape Town 8001, South Africa

ISBN: 1 877246 50 6

Managing editor: Renée Lang
Project manager: Amy Palmer
Design and production: Dexter Fry
Editor: Richard King

Colour reproduction by Colourscan (Singapore)
Printed by Tien Wah Press (Pte) Ltd

10 9 8 7 6 5 4 3 2 1

PHOTOGRAPHIC ACKNOWLEDGEMENTS

BR = Black Robin   VIP = Visual Impact Pictures
Alexander Turnbull Library, National Library of New Zealand, Te Puna Maatauranga o Aotearoa: endpapers, p4–5, 8, 18–19, 20, 21, 22, 23 (below), 24 (above), 25, 26, 27, 28 (above), 29, 30, 30–31, 32, 34, 35, 37, 38, 39, 40, 41, 42, 43, 44 (left), 57, 58, 59 (below), 60, 73, 76, 86, 87, 88, 96, 97, 98, 99, 100, 108, 109, 110–111, 112, 128, 129, 130, 131, 144, 145, 146, 147, 160, 162, 163, 178, 180, 182, 183. Auckland City Libraries (NZ): p61, 84 (right), 85. Shaun Barnett (BR): p11, 15, 48–49, 71, 95, 102 (left), 115, 116, 125, 177, 186. Peter Bush (VIP): p120. Adrian Davies (VIP): p50–51. Gareth Eyres: p1, 2–3, 6–7, 12 (left), 14 (right), 55, 62–63, 67, 84, 91 (left), 94, 101, 122–123, 124, 155, 174, 187, 188–189. Sheena Haywood (VIP): p70. Warren Jacobs: front cover, p10, 13, 90 (left), 91 (right), 143, 152–153, 165, 172–173, 175, 176, 184, 185. Glenn Jowitt: p46, 47, 66. Bob McCree: p 64 (right). National Library of Australia: back cover, p23 (top), 24 (right), 28 (right), 33, 36, 56, 59 (top), 72, 74, 75, 106, 110, 159, 161, 179, 181. New Zealand Herald: p44 (right). Darryn Pegram (BR): p79. Andy Reisinger: p103, 154. Nathan Secker (VIP): p170, 171. Graeme Sinclair (VIP): p45. Phil Suisted (Nature's Pic Images): p169. Rob Suisted (Nature's Pic Images): p12 (right), 14 (left), 16, 17, 54 (right), 64 (left), 68–69, 77, 82, 83, 89 (top), 90 (right), 92–93, 104–105, 107, 113, 114, 117, 118, 119 (left), 121, 126, 127, 134, 135, 136–137, 138–139, 140, 149 (right), 150, 150–151, 158, 166, 168, 185 (right). Philip Temple: p133, 149 (left), 157, 167. David Wall: p45 (right), 52, 53, 54 (left), 78, 80–81, 89 (below), 102 (right), 119 (right), 132, 141, 189. Phil Walter (Fotopress): p65.

FRONT COVER: *Castle Hill, Canterbury.*

BACK COVER: *The Remarkables and Lake Wakatipu, Otago. (E. Smith)*

ENDPAPERS: *Sketch map of the pastoral area of Canterbury.*

HALF-TITLE PAGE: *Dappled light on Central Otago hills.*

TITLE PAGE: *Kaikoura's coastline in the early morning.*

THIS PAGE: *Wellington Harbour, 1875. (S. Brees)*

CONTENTS PAGE: *Autumn at Arrowtown.*

Plate XXV

MAP
of the Coast of
NEW ZEALAND
discovered
in the Years 1769 and 1770,
BY I. COOK,
Commander of
His Majesty's Bark
ENDEAVOUR.

Scale of Leagues 20 to a Degree

Three Kings
CAPE MARIA VAN DIEMEN
NORTH CAPE
Sandy Bay
Knuckle Point
Doubtless Bay
Flat Point
Candle Isles
M. Camel
Point Pococke
Percy I.
C. BRETT
Poor Knights
Mr. Cuaro
THE BAY OF ISLANDS
Bream Bay
BREAM HEAD
Hen & Chickens
Malee tabeo
Barren Isles
Port Charles
THE DESERT COAST
Threantail
Pt. Rodney
C. COLVILLE
Mercury Isles
Mercury Point
Mercury Bay or Opoorangee
Court of Aldermen
Barren Point
The Mayor
White Island
CRUNAWAY
Hicks's Bay
False Bay
RIVER THAMES
Town Pt.
Mentchera
EHEINOMAUWE
Flat Island
BAY OF PLENTY
C. EAST
East Isd.
Woody Head
Gennet Island
Albatros Point
Lowland Point
Lowland Bay
Highland Point
Mount Edgcombe
Tegadoo
Tolaga
Parkinson Isd.
Gable end fore Id.
Tettua motu
Made the Coast the 5th of October 1769
Sugar Loaf Isles
Sugar Loaf Point
POVERTY BAY
or TAGNERUA
Young Nicks head
HAWKES BAY
Table Cape
Terakoko
Left the Coast the 31st of March 1770.
CAPE EGMONT
Mount Egmont
Teahoway or Portland I.
C. KIDNAPPERS
Bare Island
COOK'S
CAPE FAREWELL
Rocks Point
Blind Bay
C. STEPHENS
CUTTERAWITTE BAY
Black Head
C. Turnagain
ADMIRALTY BAY
Totarranoe Country
Castle Point
Flat Point
CAPE PALLISER
CAPE FOULWIND
CHARLOTTE'S SOUND
or Cannibal Bay
Snowy Mountains
Cloudy Bay
CAPE CAMPBELL
STRAITS
Lookers on
TOAI POONAMOO
Gore's Bay
BANKS'S ISLAND
Open Bay
THE SOUTHERN ALPS
Cascades Point
Mistaken Bay
Doubtfull Harbour
C. SAUNDERS
Five Fingers Point
Dusky Bay
WEST CAPE
SOLANDERS I.
S.W. Bay
Moulineux's Harbour
S.E. Bay
Bench I.
CAPE SOUTH
The Traps

Longitude West from the Meridian of Greenwich

The dotted Line shews the Ship's Track.
Part of the Coast left unfinished has
not been explored.
☩ This Mark shews where the
Endeavour anchored.
+ Rocks.

B. Longmate sculpsit

Cape Reinga

Northland to Waikato

Kaitaia

Kerikeri • Russell
• *Bay of Islands*

Dargaville • • **Whangarei**

Great Barrier Island

Kaipara Harbour *Hauraki Gulf*

• Coromandel

Coromandel Peninsula

AUCKLAND •

T A S M A N S E A

N O R T H I S L A N D

Hamilton • • **Tauranga**

East Coast & Hawke's Bay

East Cape

Taranaki & King Country

Te Kuiti • • **Rotorua**

Te Urewera National Park

• **Taupo**

Lake Taupo

New Plymouth •

Taranaki/Mt Egmont National Park

Tongariro National Park

• **Gisborne**

Taranaki/Mt Egmont

Whanganui National Park

Hawke Bay

• **Napier**

Hastings

Wanganui •

Bay of Plenty & Volcanic Plateau

Nelson & Marlborough

Wellington & Wairarapa

Farewell Spit

Palmerston North •

Kapiti Island

Takaka • *Abel Tasman National Park*

Kahurangi National Park

Marlborough Sounds

• Masterton

Nelson • Picton •

Cook Strait

• **WELLINGTON**

Blenheim •

West Coast

Westport •

Nelson Lakes National Park

S O U T H I S L A N D

Paparoa National Park

• Kaikoura

Greymouth •

Arthurs Pass National Park

Hokitika •

Franz Josef •

Westland/Tai Poutini National Park

Aoraki/Mt Cook National Park

• **CHRISTCHURCH**

Banks Peninsula

• Akaroa

Aoraki/Mt Cook

Haast •

Canterbury

S O U T H P A C I F I C O C E A N

Mt Aspiring National Park

• Timaru

Milford Sound

• Wanaka

• **Queenstown** • Oamaru

• Alexandra

Fiordland National Park

• Te Anau

• **DUNEDIN**

• **Invercargill**

• Bluff

Foveaux Strait

STEWART ISLAND

Otago & Southland

INTRODUCTION

'LAST, LONELIEST, LOVELIEST ...'

S O RUDYARD KIPLING wrote of Auckland more than a century ago. But his eulogy applies easily to the entire windswept, sea-hemmed stretch of the 'Happy Isles' of Aotearoa New Zealand, so far from the rest of the world that they are less a part of it than its model. They form an exemplar of its landscapes and, on a planet increasingly burned, ravaged and poisoned, a South Pacific life-raft for ancient forests and pristine waters with skies that remain cerulean blue. For New Zealand was indeed the 'last and loneliest' habitable corner of the world for human contact, far enough away from continents to be last found, last settled, last damaged . . .

New Zealand contains so many landscapes because its surface is so new – the shaping from fold and buckle, slippage and earthquake, eruption and erosion is so recent, so *now*. Its oldest rocks are a mere 600 million years old, when the oldest on earth are aged four or five billion. As a distinct entity, New Zealand started about 80 million years ago, rifting from the supercontinent Gondwana. It drifted away east, rising and falling in the primordial Pacific, stretching out sideways, dry and cold during ice ages, wet and tropical when the planet warmed.

New Zealand's final shape and attitude has been governed by its position astride the junction of two tectonic plates. The Pacific Plate to the east dips under the Indo–Australian Plate to the west as this slides north-east. A glance at the map clearly shows this juncture in the south-west to north-east uplift of the Southern Alps and North Island ranges along the line of the great Alpine and central North Island fault system. Rocks in north-west Nelson match rocks in Fiordland –

PRECEDING PAGES: *Then and now. The first chart of New Zealand, prepared by Captain James Cook in 1770, compares well with a modern map prepared with the aid of trigonometrical survey and earth-satellite technology.*

LEFT: *The head of Queen Charlotte Sound, Marlborough.*

ABOVE: *Schist boulders, Whitcombe River, West Coast.*

ABOVE: *White Island, or Whakaari, New Zealand's most continuously active volcano, lies 50 kilometres off the coast of the Bay of Plenty. Its crater is a maelstrom of steam plumes, gas vents, sulphuric acid holes and boiling pools.*

RIGHT: *The volcanic heart of the North Island. Beyond the colourful lakes of Tongariro lie Lake Rotoaira and, further still, New Zealand's greatest lake, Taupo, formed by a cataclysmic explosion nearly 2000 years ago.*

clear evidence of the sideways slide along this line. The fault system is the source of many of New Zealand's earthquakes – the highway along the harbour edge between the capital city Wellington and Lower Hutt follows its line, running over land raised by an 1855 quake.

Volcanic activity has been another major shaping force along the junction of the plates, especially from the centre of the North Island, trending north-east and out to sea, part of the Pacific 'Ring of Fire'. The last cataclysmic eruption was the explosion that created New Zealand's largest lake, Taupo, around AD 150 – an event recorded in the skies of imperial Rome and which covered the core of the North Island in ash. White Island, Ruapehu and Ngauruhoe still rumble, smoke and discharge. Taranaki/Mount Egmont may be dormant, and the small cones around which Auckland city is built may be extinct, but it is only a matter of (geological) time before the land explodes somewhere again or makes a major shift. Signs that the action is still going on, that the geological furniture is always being rearranged, are earthquakes that regularly rattle china in city cafés, volcanoes that periodically jet ash over the countryside, and the top falling off Aoraki/Mount Cook.

At the time of writing, however, New Zealand comprises two largish islands, the North Island and the one-third-larger South Island, plus a much smaller Stewart Island and numerous offshore islands. All these nominally cover 270,000 square kilometres, rather more than the United Kingdom and rather less than Italy. But since three-quarters of it is hill or mountain country

above 200 metres in altitude, its actual surface area is much greater. New Zealand reaches a peak at Mount Cook's 3753 metres, stretches more than 1600 kilometres through 34 to 47° south of the equator, and has a coastline extending 5650 kilometres, greater than that of the United States. The country is narrow-gutted, with no inland locality more than 120 kilometres from the sea.

New Zealand is 2000 kilometres away from the nearest continental landmass, Australia, the largest left-over from old Gondwana. This is almost as far as from London to Moscow – the width of Europe – or Seattle to San Diego – the north–south span of the United States. In keeping with this scale of remoteness, New Zealand's own farthest away offshore islands, the Chathams, lie 870 kilometres to the east.

High and narrow, stretching from the subtropics to the subantarctic, New Zealand presented, when it had drifted deep into the southern Pacific, an irritating barrier to prevailing westerly

ABOVE: *The roof of New Zealand. The sunlit-and-shadowed south ridge of Mount Sefton (3157 metres) marks the Main Divide of the Southern Alps and the junction of Aoraki/ Mount Cook and Westland/Tai Poutini National Parks, the northern plinth of Te Wahipounamu World Heritage Area. Sefton's summit points to Aoraki/Mount Cook (3753 metres).*

ABOVE: *New Zealand's temperate rainforests harbour some of the most ancient tree forms on the planet.*

RIGHT: *The ancestry of* Nothofagus *beech forests can be traced back 135 million years.*

winds. They whistled round the world largely unimpeded before striking the islands' mountain ranges and dumping copious volumes of rain. This, and a cool to mild temperature range, generated rich vegetative growth, even at high altitude. During ice ages, when sea levels dropped and higher regions were glaciated, forest still grew in favoured coastal margins, waiting for warmer eras when it could recolonise barren lands.

In these forests were some of the most ancient tree types on earth. *Podocarpus* conifers, kauri and *Nothofagus* southern beech have ancestries going back 135 million years to Gondwana. Pollen and leaf fossils of *Nothofagus*, for example, have been found in Antarctica, and living New Zealand beeches have cousins in Tasmania and southern South America. Beeches growing in the Upper Cretaceous period, 100 million years ago, were such direct ancestors of New Zealand's silver beech that fossil pollen grains from that ancient time are indistinguishable from pollen of today's trees. New Zealand's land forms may be young, but much of its living biota is the most ancient on earth, making the country, as ecologist David Bellamy once described it, a 'Moa's Ark' adrift in the South Pacific.

By about 10,000 years ago, three-quarters of New Zealand was covered in conifer–hardwood forest. The predominant coniferous species were podocarps such as totara, kahikatea and rimu, while the mighty kauri, the largest tree by timber volume in the world, dominated forests north of latitude 38. The prevailing hardwoods, especially in the south and at altitude, were southern beech, along with rata and kamahi. There were extensive wetlands about coastal estuaries and, in some dry eastern locations, areas of short tussock grasslands. Above the bushline, widespread tall tussock grasslands sheltered unique subalpine flowering plants.

ABOVE: *A group of kahikatea* (Dacrycarpus dacrydioides), *New Zealand's dominant swampland tree, and tallest, sometimes reaching 60 metres in height.*

LEFT: *The mighty kauri* (Agathis australis), *the native conifer that once dominated the forests of the northern North Island. The largest trees, by timber volume, in the world, most were felled during the century to 1920 to build ships and the houses of early Auckland.*

ABOVE: *The unfolding frond of a tree fern. Transformed into the figurative koru, it inspires much Maori art.*

RIGHT: *The emblem of New Zealand, the kiwi. There are three species of this ancient flightless bird (here* Apteryx australis*), whose ancestry dates back to the time New Zealand broke away from the supercontinent Gondwana 80 million years ago.*

New Zealand's tree ferns are even older than podocarp or beech, dating from 200 million years ago, and would have graced Jurassic parklands. After that age of dinosaurs – of which New Zealand had its share – mammals became the dominant animal force on the planet. But by that time New Zealand was so far offshore from Gondwana that none made it to the shaky isles except, later, a few species of small bats that winged in on the westerlies. New birds came over that way, too, to join the strange descendants of pterosaurian times that had grown up here, most of them not bothering to fly in the absence of mammalian predators. Moa, the biggest birds that have ever lived anywhere, had for so long had no notions of flying that their skeletons show no trace of wing bones. There were a dozen species of moa, ranging from the size of large turkeys to giants two and a half metres tall and weighing 230 kilograms. There was a variety of kiwis, too – flightless, nocturnal, short-sighted, with nostrils on the end of their beaks and laying eggs half their body weight. Another bird that gave up flying, and dashed about in the night to avoid the attentions of falcons and eagles, was the kakapo, the largest and heaviest parrot in the world. Long isolation bred peculiar character traits in New Zealand birds, and even relative newcomers from over the waves came to learn that flying was often a waste of time and energy.

Before humans – that scourge of the natural world – turned up less than a thousand years ago, this is the way New Zealand had been for many millennia following the last glacial

climactic. Long isolation meant there were only about 2000 native species of vascular plants (Japan has twice that number), but more than 80 per cent of these were endemic. Similarly, while there were only about 130 species of land birds, most of these were endemic. About 80 species of sea birds bred along the coasts and fed in lagoons, and the seas were rich in fish, crustaceans and marine megafauna such as seals, whales and dolphins. When the first humans turned up, although the mountainous and heavily forested interior was gloomy and forbidding, there was plenty to eat along the coast.

Polynesians arrived between the eleventh and fourteenth centuries during the last phase of their exploration and settlement of islands in the Pacific bowl. The Polynesian migration had begun some 3000 years earlier when voyagers moved out of Melanesia in a progressive eastward movement that took them to the central Pacific islands as far as Tahiti and the Marquesas.

ABOVE: *Hector's dolphin* (Cephalorhynchus hectori). *New Zealand's coastal waters are frequented by many cetaceans (whales, dolphins and porpoises), but only this one, the world's smallest, is endemic.*

Subsequent voyages took them north to Hawaii and as far south-east as Rapa Nui (Easter Island). Linguistic and cultural evidence suggests that the Polynesians who became the Maori of New Zealand arrived from the Rarotongan (Cook Islands) region.

Given that prevailing winds make it difficult to sail south-west from Rarotonga to New Zealand, accidental discovery is unlikely. The first navigators probably came here by design, looking for new islands whose presence had been indicated by such natural signs as seasonally migrating birds, in particular the long-tailed cuckoo, which annually arrived in the Rarotonga region in March and departed again in October to breed in New Zealand. The cuckoo migration pattern follows the most favourable wind periods for sailing to and from New Zealand and the islands of eastern Polynesia. The first Maori probably encountered New Zealand as 'Aotearoa', a long white cloud across the ranges of the northern North Island, and sailed somewhere into the natural landfall arc between East Cape and North Cape.

It is not yet clear, and may never be, whether the first discoverers were also the first settlers or if the explorers returned to the Rarotongan islands with the news of a large uninhabited land, and this led to a considered and successive migration of several groups. But by the end of the fourteenth century settlement was established at many locations from the Far North to the Deep

LEFT: *Warriors in the Bay of Islands wait for favourable winds before undertaking a hostile expedition by waka to the Thames region. One waka is more than 20 metres long. By this time, the late 1830s, most men are armed with muskets although traditional taiaha are present. (A. Earle)*

South of Aotearoa, especially along the more sheltered and navigable eastern coastlines. Heaviest Maori settlement has always been concentrated in the mostly frost-free regions north of latitude 38 and on the North Island's upper east coast. These areas were obviously the most climatically salubrious to a neolithic people without access to hides and textiles, and provided conditions most favourable for the growing of the tropical food plants they brought with them, in particular the kumara (sweet potato). They also brought with them the first land mammals – the kiore (Polynesian rat) as a food source, and the kuri, a now-extinct barkless dog.

It has been estimated that when Captain Cook arrived in 1769, three-quarters of all Maori lived in those upper North Island regions, and only five per cent in the South Island. For a time, however, the latter had supported a much higher percentage of the early settlers. The first travellers to the South Island discovered a major food and bone source in the large populations of moa inhabiting its eastern grasslands and open forest, as well as numerous and dense colonies of seals along the coast. These early New Zealanders brought about the first major ecological changes by human agency. Over a period of no more than two to three hundred years as many as half a million moa were killed, until this bird family became extinct.

In the course of hunting, deliberate and accidental fires caused the destruction of vast areas

ABOVE: *This canoe prow from the early 1840s illustrates the high level of creativity and skill attained by Maori carvers in the pre-European period. (S. Brees)*

of forest, so that most of the plains and downlands on the eastern side of the Southern Alps were transformed into scrub and grasslands. It is estimated that about a quarter of New Zealand's forest cover was destroyed during the 500 years following first settlement, by a population that had reached a peak of no more than 150,000 by the late eighteenth century. With the moa and forest went other bird species as well, around 30 in all. Hunting pressure on seals effectively eliminated them from the North Island, confining larger populations to the south and west of the South Island.

As the duration of Polynesian settlement and population increased, the economy of the first New Zealanders shifted from the initial phases of opportunistic exploitation to a more conservative and sympathetic use of resources. While hunting, fishing and gathering remained vital to survival, seasonal management ensured wiser use of natural food sources in conjunction with a garden agriculture that developed to produce and store harvests of imported plants in a more difficult and unpredictable climate. With increasing isolation and then disjunction from the Pacific homeland, local adaptations of customary Polynesian beliefs, myths and social behaviour developed into a distinctive and settled culture that responded to the unique natural world on which they depended. This was most vividly expressed in a wood-carving art without peer among neolithic cultures that arose from a growing spiritual relationship with the resources of the great forests around them. This artistic skill was transferred splendidly into stone after the discovery of nephrite jade (greenstone/pounamu) in the west of the South Island, the greatest treasure of pre-European New Zealand.

Communities grew up mostly around favourable gardening lands and productive birding and

ABOVE: *A re-creation of alarm and call to arms inside a fortified pa, showing conch shell, wooden trumpet and hand weapons. (J.McDonald)*

LEFT: *A Maori pa, or fortified village, on Motuara Island in Queen Charlotte Sound, at the time of early European contact. (J. Webber)*

fishing locations in the regions surrounding the North Island 'landfall arc'. The kainga (hamlet) provided the home focus for the whanau (family), which claimed close kinship with a group of connecting families in a hapu (clan). As territorial boundaries became more settled, defined by obvious geographical features such as river or mountain, as well as marriage loyalties among whanau and hapu, there developed an increasing corporate sense of iwi, the tribe or nation within a self-contained world of Aotearoa (this name was not universally used).

In such a large world, with its infinite possibilities, there was no need to explore for any other, and trans-ocean voyaging skills were subsumed by the need for coasting skills and the development of techniques that were of use not just for gardening and carving but also for defending hapu and iwi land (whenua), property and possessions (taonga). Some of this whenua and taonga became more precious and desirable than others, and conflicts developed between the new nations, much as they had in other countries on other continents. As always, much might be settled by strategic marriages and generous treaties, but greed, revenge (utu), feud and simple belligerence fuelled cycles of war. The pa (fortified village) was developed, together with a variety of hand weapons vital in a warrior culture based on close-quarter fighting.

By the mid-eighteenth century all of the land was known to the different iwi, from the cliffy headlands of Te Reinga in the Far North, to the volcanic deserts of Tongariro, to the bays of stormswept Raukawa (Cook Strait) between the islands, to the passes over the south's icy mountains to the sounds and isles of rainy Murihiku in the Deep South. A rich and complex society had grown up within the constraints of a solely oral culture and neolithic technology, and its mythology told of how the great Polynesian discoverer Maui had ventured deep in this southern

ABOVE: *An imaginative depiction of Polynesian demi-god Maui fishing up the North Island – Te Ika a Maui – from his South Island canoe. (W. Dittmer)*

RIGHT: *Abel Janszoon Tasman (1603–59), explorer for the Dutch East India Company, was the first European to discover New Zealand, in December 1642. He described it as 'a large land, uplifted high' and the edge of a southern continent.*

ocean. From his canoe (South Island), with Stewart Island as his anchorstone, he fished up the North Island (Te Ika a Maui) to create a new world for a people who had no collective name for all who lived in this most isolated of lands but who knew themselves by the names of their new nations. However, it had been prophesied that a ship with the wings of a giant sea bird would one day come carrying men with pale skins who would change this world forever. They would cause the first New Zealanders to define themselves as Maori, tangata whenua, natives of this land.

The first squaresail wings of European voyagers to arrive off the coast belonged to the small exploring ships of Abel Janszoon Tasman, half a world from home, as he searched for precious minerals, timber and other trading resources that might be of value to his masters in the Dutch East India Company. He had already discovered Tasmania on a long voyage east from Mauritius, and his tiny flotilla made the first-known navigation of the Tasman Sea to raise up 'a large land, uplifted high' – the west coast of the South Island – on 13 December 1642. He thought he had reached 'Staten Landt' (Chile) on the far shore of the Pacific, but did not test this conclusion by thorough exploration. He was discouraged by the killing of four of his men by Maori while his ships were anchored in Taitapu (Golden Bay). Tasman sailed on east until encountering the Manawatu coast of the North Island but did not prove the strait between the islands, or even that

the country consisted of islands, retaining the impression, as he sailed away off the west coast of the North Island, that he was tracking the coast of a continent. Dutch authorities later considered that Tasman had not proved his discovery as part of Staten Landt and so called it 'Niuew Zeeland', new sea land.

When James Cook sailed south from Tahiti in August 1769, under British Admiralty instructions to search for a great southern continent, said to lie somewhere below 40° South, he knew of Tasman's discovery of a landmass at that latitude. His two-month voyage across the South Pacific slowly proved there was no extensive landmass east of Tasman's 'Staten Landt'. Cook's navigation was aided by the new and marvellous Harrison's clock – the most reliable timepiece yet invented – and he fetched up off the east coast of the North Island at latitude 39 South and longitude 178 East on 6 October.

Cook's first encounter with the native people of Turanganui (Poverty Bay) reflected Tasman's experience of a 'warlike people', but the casualties this time were several Maori killed and wounded. The clash was tragic but on the single 33-metre-long barque *Endeavour*, 96 naval officers, scientists and crew were as far away from home and aid as it was possible to be. Cook's first responsibility was the security and welfare of his ship and men, on which depended the successful accomplishment of his multi-faceted mission, which included charting this new land's coastline and making the first survey of its inhabitants and natural attributes. Cook proved a much superior navigator and commander than Tasman, and during the remainder of his

TOP: *This idealistic re-creation of Cook's landing in 1769 shows friendly curiosity during the first encounter between European and Maori, with Cook as the bringer of the fruits of civilisation. (E. Temple)*

ABOVE: *Captain James Cook (1728–79) made three voyages of exploration to New Zealand.*

ABOVE: *Sir Joseph Banks (1743–1820), naturalist on Cook's first South Pacific voyage, oversaw the collection of thousands of native plants and animals. Later, he was president of the Royal Society.*
(J. Russell)

RIGHT: *South Island Maori at the time of early European contact. This scene was painted by John Webber during Cook's third voyage, and his last visit to Ship Cove, Queen Charlotte Sound.*
(J. Webber)

six-month stay in New Zealand waters he was able to establish mostly workable relations with other Maori the expedition encountered.

Captain Cook made the first complete circumnavigation of the islands, producing a remarkably accurate chart. His scientists, led by Joseph Banks, collected thousands of natural specimens new to European science; his artists created the first images of the land and its people. The findings of this voyage, and Cook's two further expeditions to New Zealand in 1773 and 1777, placed the country firmly on European maps and pulled a new world, its resources and possibilities, within the ambit of European scientists, missionaries and traders.

It was the Age of Enlightenment and of revolution, yielding new political and humanistic philosophies. It was also the start of the Industrial Revolution, science producing new technologies and goods that would need increasing volumes of raw materials and growing markets, as well as land to settle the enlarging populations that would both produce and consume. While Europeans like James Cook could feel understanding and compassion for the condition and prospects of indigenous peoples such as the Maori, this was at best paternalistic. The *Holy Bible*, Harrison's clock and the *Endeavour*'s Royal Ordnance cannon were confirmation enough for them of the superiority and irresistible power of European civilisation.

The collision of cultures that followed Cook's voyages was to prove as wrenching to both New

Zealand's natural life and Maori society as the collision of tectonic plates was to its landscape, but over a much shorter period of time. Although few Europeans arrived in New Zealand to settle in the 70 years after Cook's rediscovery, the exploitation of the country's resources began almost immediately, as did the introduction of animals and artefacts that saw Maori shift overnight from the stone to the iron age.

By 1800 the Bay of Islands had become a favourite base for whalers, and sealers had arrived on New Zealand's southern coasts after their decimation of the rookeries in Australia's Bass Strait. By 1820 this industry had collapsed from overslaughter and changing fashions. So had the sperm whale population. Hunting for the southern right whale continued from South Island shore stations for another 135 years, though returns from this industry faded rapidly after 1835. From the 1790s British naval ships visited Coromandel for spar timber, but the Hokianga district saw the first significant timber industry after Sydney merchants began establishing sawpits for kauri in 1820. Dressed flax ('New Zealand hemp') was also in demand, for rope- and sailmaking. By the

ABOVE: *Whaling and sealing, for oil products and skins, were the major extractive industries during the first half of the nineteenth century. This engraving from the* Illustrated London News *in 1847 shows the death, or 'flurry', of a sperm whale in the 'South Sea fishery'.*

ABOVE: *Hongi Hika, the famous Nga Puhi warrior (1772–1828) who first recognised the power of the European musket in tribal wars. During the decade before his death – from a musket wound – his warriors defeated and slaughtered adversaries throughout the upper North Island.*

RIGHT: *Kororareka (Russell) in the Bay of Islands, about 1840. Sixteen ships are shown at anchor, reflecting the fact that, until the mid-1840s, the bay was New Zealand's major port of call for traders and whalers. (L. Le Breton)*

1840s the kauri forests had been cleared well back from the shorelines of the Bay of Islands, Whangaroa and Hokianga.

Consequently, the sparsely populated South Island and the more densely populated and cultivated region of Northland were the first to feel the impact of European – mainly British – contact. At first Maori were in control, superior in numbers, secure in their place in the land and eager to acquire the iron and steel tools and other domestic goods that the white strangers – Pakeha – traded for timber, flax, fresh food and the recreational favours of Maori women. Pakeha brought new crops, too, like potatoes. The first missionaries in 1814 introduced wheat, other grains, root and green vegetables and stone fruit. To the pigs and goats that Cook and other navigators had released, they added horses, cows, domestic poultry and the first sheep. New rats came ashore, and the dogs and cats to chase them. The first rabbits arrived in the 1830s.

Kororareka, in the sheltered Bay of Islands, became one of the busiest ports in the Pacific, and it was here that alcohol began to flow in killing quantities, here that diseases foreign to the Maori immune system struck hard, and here, in 1807, that the first firearms changed hands. Nga Puhi tribesmen from the northern region first recognised the power of the musket and traded for them with a passion that led to chief Hongi Hika in 1821 leading an army of 3000 warriors armed with a thousand guns to exact utu from old enemies in the south. A thousand Ngati Paoa were slain in Tamaki (Auckland), 1500 died in the Waikato, and Hongi's men continued on their bloody way for another half-dozen years. Soon all iwi clamoured for muskets, for assault or defence, and in 1831 alone, 6000 were shipped in by Sydney traders.

The musket wars that continued into the 1830s were said to have accounted for the death of up to 30,000 people. It is more likely that this number, more than a quarter of the Maori population, were displaced by the wars. Ten thousand may have died, but not only by musket shot. Tuberculosis, measles and venereal disease played their part, too, as well as booze, tobacco and changed and unhealthy living conditions caused by new concentrations of populations in swampy coastal littorals, close to the flax plants that gave Maori the vital barter product for ever more muskets, so completing the most vicious of circles.

The influence of missionaries of various Christian denominations was limited in the first dozen years after their arrival, and there were few converts. But the death and dislocation of the musket wars caused increasing numbers of lower-caste Maori to find consolation and security in Christianity's peaceful moralities and rituals. The missionaries also traded with desirable goods, and many settled permanently. They actively encouraged Maori to learn and adopt new agricultural techniques and food plants, and introduced the written and printed word. All of this began to undermine old beliefs and traditions, weakening Maori society more radically than a hundred thousand muskets.

By the mid-1830s Maori society was coming under severe stress. The musket wars had disrupted the old balances of power across the North Island. The missionary hold on hearts and minds was strengthening, while non-missionary Pakeha settlement was increasing, giving rise to disorder and anarchy on the New Zealand frontier. The British government had little interest in

ABOVE: *A Maori taua (war party) with muskets performing a haka outside Maketu Pa in the Bay of Plenty. Although this watercolour was painted during the Land Wars of the 1860s, it represents well the fearsome sight that met North Island iwi as Hongi Hika's warriors invaded in the 1820s. (H. Robley)*

ABOVE: *Edward Gibbon Wakefield (1796–1862) as a young man. His planned settlement theories, propaganda and behind-the-scenes management strongly influenced the activities of the New Zealand Company and associated bodies that led to the founding of the Wellington, Nelson, New Plymouth, Otago and Canterbury settlements between 1839 and 1852. (A. Wivell)*

RIGHT: *The baptism of Te Ati Awa chief Te Puni in Rangiatea church, Otaki in 1853. Two years before this, land commissioner Donald McLean had written, 'Christianity is one of the principal causes of our easy conquest and retention of the New Zealand islands.' More than any number of muskets, the teachings of Christian evangelism fatally weakened traditional Maori belief, custom and social structure. (C. Barraud)*

annexing New Zealand, but the influence of evangelical humanitarians at the Colonial Office meant that news of lawlessness and conflict with the Maori gave it cause to listen to missionary pleas for Britain to establish the law and order of the Crown.

Concurrently, another major force was gathering way: speculative associations that believed New Zealand was ideal in land and climate for the establishment of British migrant settlements. Pre-eminent was the New Zealand Company under the philosophical guidance and political management of colonial theoriser Edward Gibbon Wakefield, who urged planned settlements that would transport all the best elements of English rural and urban society to this new land. This would see the creation of a Britain of the South Seas, providing raw produce for British industries and an expanding market for their finished goods, helping Britain to become the 'workshop of the world'.

In the late 1830s a struggle developed between the Church Missionary Society (CMS) and the New Zealand Company for the favour of British politicians and administrators over the fate of New Zealand. The missionaries wished not wholesale settlement, but to make the Maori brown Christians under benevolent British rule. The government dithered but was eventually forced to concede that British settlement was inevitable and that all interests would be served best by making the country a Crown colony in a way that protected Maori interests.

While the Wakefield-inspired Company had helped to force the government's hand, it was frustrated in its attempt to gain a pre-eminent role in annexation. The Company's economic theory also depended on its buying New Zealand land cheap and selling dear, to bankroll

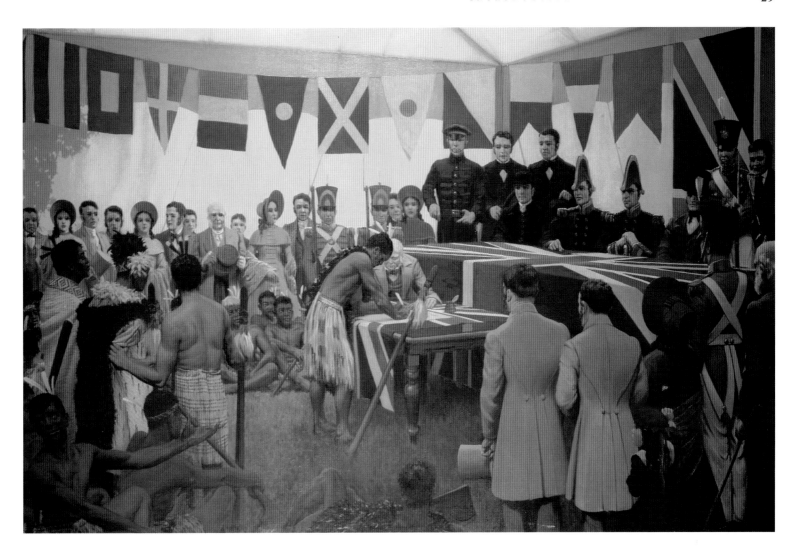

immigration and investment, and government plans threatened this. The Company sent off an expedition in mid-1839 to secure as much land as possible from Maori before Crown law was established. This expedited government plans to send Captain William Hobson to New Zealand as Lieutenant-Governor designate. But by the time Hobson arrived in the Bay of Islands at the end of January 1840, Wakefield's younger brother William had treated for vast areas of land in the Cook Strait region and the Company's first migrant ships had arrived to establish the settlement of Wellington. The fatal conflicts that arose from this situation were caused by a government that had failed to act early and decisively enough.

Hobson arrived with a set of instructions from the Colonial Office, firm advice from his immediate superior, the Governor of New South Wales, and ideas of his own. CMS missionaries sought to strongly influence all of these and were in a powerful position as the principal linguistic intermediaries between Hobson and local Maori chiefs. Under some pressure, which included Company activities in the south and an inflated threat of potential French annexation, the Lieutenant-Governor put together a treaty inside a week and at Waitangi on 6 February began the process of securing chiefly signatures to it from throughout New Zealand.

ABOVE: *A reconstruction of the signing of the Treaty of Waitangi in February 1840, enabling New Zealand to become a British Crown colony while safeguarding Maori land and property rights. Its preamble and three clauses, in both Maori and English, were put together within a week, and their exact meaning and interpretation have remained subjects of dispute ever since. (M. King)*

ABOVE: *Captain William Hobson (1792–1842), first Lieutenant-Governor of New Zealand and architect of the Treaty of Waitangi. (J. McDonald)*

RIGHT: *'The emigrant's farewell. The Lord be with you!' The distress of family parting as emigrants prepare to make the long voyage from England to start a new life in a colony on the other side of the world. For many British emigrants to New Zealand, separation from family and home was final. (J. Fagan)*

From the outset the three apparently simple clauses of the Treaty of Waitangi – in English and Maori – held different meanings to different people, and have continued to do so for more than 160 years. A prominent witness to the proceedings, missionary printer William Colenso, seriously doubted if Waitangi Maori understood its real import – to make New Zealand a colony with sovereignty vested in the British Crown; Maori to be accorded the rights and responsibilities of British citizens, including protection of their property. Part of the latter undertaking included, as an apparent protection, the provision that Maori sales of land could take place only through Crown agency, and not in deals with private speculators.

The formal establishment of the country's new status came in May 1840, five months before the Treaty was ratified in London. When news reached Hobson of Wellington settlement's move to establish its own rule of law, he declared New Zealand a Crown colony before many more signatures to the Treaty had reached him; and none from the South Island, which he claimed by right of discovery. Whatever the intent of the Treaty, as French explorer Dumont d'Urville observed at the time, New Zealand had been set on an irrevocable course of Europeanisation.

The New Zealand Company established further settlements at Wanganui, Nelson and New Plymouth, but a Crown land commission disallowed most of its pre-Treaty 'purchases' and the

Company eventually folded as the basis for its speculative success was removed. The Wakefield plan as a self-contained colonial package proved impracticable, both financially and socially, on such a distant and pioneering frontier, and without a sound export market. Yet it did establish the principles of funded and organised migration of skilled and responsible settlers, determined on the founding of a new life and society that were to guide the future massive colonisations of not only New Zealand but also other British dominions such as Australia and Canada. The Company also established the sites of many of the major cities and towns of New Zealand and brought in the first substantial numbers of settlers, many of whom became future political leaders of the colony.

Although the Company failed, Wakefield persisted in attempting to realise his colonial theories by encouraging South Island planned settlements held together not only by investment in land and the transportation of a model society, but also by the glue of religious faith and nostalgia. The Free Church of Scotland settlement in Otago (1848) stumbled, but the Church of England enterprise, Canterbury (1850), proved to be the most successful of the Wakefield-inspired settlements, owing to the quality of its backers and leaders and a geographically favourable site that allowed for the rapid expansion of pastoral sheep farming beyond the colony's surveyed blocks.

For even ideal Canterbury could not survive within the town and country limits of the Wakefield model. Cash and growth depended not on controlled self-sufficiency but successful exporting to the home markets of Britain, and this early period of settlement coincided with spectacular growth in the English textile industry and its insatiable demand for wool. Canterbury led the way as the New Zealand economy rode into the future on the sheep's back, exporting to a

market on the opposite side of the world. Wakefield's vision of imperial economics, the capital tie between mother country and colony, was being fulfilled.

The early and major exception to the Wakefield settlements was Auckland, which Hobson had chosen for the site of his capital. Located on the southern shore of the Waitemata Harbour, it was central both to the main Maori population and to an easy seaborne communications system between the Bay of Plenty and Bay of Islands. Compared with all the Wakefield settlements before Canterbury, it also had an accessible and fertile hinterland. Ironically, during its early years the prosperous town of Auckland, serving and served by a productive and ordered countryside, was the perfect Wakefield model. As the centre of government administration and the focus of shipping and trading for the upper North Island, it became the wealthiest and largest New Zealand settlement by the late 1840s.

During the 20 years following the Treaty of Waitangi and the first planned settlements, the economic and social matrix was created that was to govern the growth and development of New Zealand both nationally and internationally for more than a century. Land, its ownership and use, was the central issue. The increasing British population viewed most of the land as 'waste' or unused, something to be cleared, cultivated and profited from. Maori saw land as held

ABOVE: *Governor Hobson established his capital at Auckland on the Waitemata Harbour in 1841. This view, painted 20 years later, looks out from the grounds of Government House to North Head and Rangitoto Island. The city, indicated at right, quickly became the most populous in New Zealand and, during the twentieth century, the country's chief business and industrial centre.*

ABOVE: *Trading, farming and business enterprises during the early days of European settlement were often joint undertakings between Pakeha and Maori, or were dependent on Maori labour and services. Thom's whaling station and nearby inn and ferry service at Paremata, north of Wellington, was a joint enterprise based on intermarriage and local hapu protection. (S. Brees)*

communally for the benefit of the controlling iwi, and had no concept of capitalist individual ownership. At first Maori regarded 'selling' land more as the granting of a lease of use. Even when the true meaning of 'sale' was appreciated, the initially small numbers of Pakeha settlers appeared no threat. Maori retained the physical upper hand and benefited from supplying the new settlements with food and labour, learning to operate mills and trading ships, without all of which Pakeha would not have survived.

But the Maori population declined and the Pakeha population increased, to parity by 1858 and then quickly to a majority, bringing an endless demand for more land, not just for direct clearance for farming but also for capitalist speculation. Maori discovered that government preemption in land sales meant profit to government and a system that intrinsically favoured the settlers. The increasing transfer of land meant loss of mana, loss of turangawaewae (domicile), loss of taonga. Additionally, there was an inherent racism in settler assumptions of civilised superiority and their disapproval of 'savage practices' and behaviour, though Maori could not match Pakeha for material greed and social arrogance.

As the European population began to outstrip the Maori, and the main settlements expanded, the demands for self-government grew, and in 1852 the New Zealand Constitution Act was passed by the British Parliament to allow the new colony a General Assembly consisting of a Governor, a Legislative Council (an upper appointed house, abolished in 1950) and a House of Representatives empowered to make laws that were 'not repugnant to the laws of England'. On this point the British government continued to oversee and even disallow New Zealand legislation for many years, and full responsible self-government was not completely effective until 1891.

Ties with the mother country remained strong, and it was not until 1947 that New Zealand finally took the powers to amend its own constitution and pass laws that might be inconsistent with Britain's. During the early period of developing self-government, New Zealand also had a system of provincial government that recognised the physical separation of the new settlements and the distinct character and needs of each. The provinces lasted until 1876, when Prime Minister Julius Vogel succeeded in centralising political and administrative power in the capital Wellington.

Similar self-governing changes were being made in other British dominions such as Canada and Australia; just as there had been similar treaties to the Treaty of Waitangi with native peoples in North America; just as the great wave of European colonisation and exploitation was sweeping over all the lightly inhabited regions of the world, causing social and physical change on a scale and at a speed never before witnessed in human history. The experience for Maori, and for the New Zealand landscape, was both typical and a minor part of nineteenth-century imperialism. During the century between the end of the Napoleonic Wars and the start of the First World War, 50 million people left Europe for lives in the new worlds. Of these, 60 per cent went to the United States, only 5 per cent to Australia and less than one per cent came to New Zealand.

ABOVE: *Christchurch and the Avon River in 1861 from a tower of the new Provincial Council Building, constructed during the heyday of provincial government.*

Conflict over land sales brought war between British settlers and Maori in Taranaki, the Waikato and Bay of Plenty during the 1860s. Maori inflicted a severe defeat on British troops and militia when they attacked the formidable Gate Pa near Tauranga in April 1864.

RIGHT: *The British forces gained revenge in overcoming the incomplete defences of Te Ranga two months later. (S. Calvert)*

ABOVE: *Peace was finally made in the Tauranga region at Te Papa camp. (M. Jackson)*

A small number to a small and distant land. Yet half a million migrants in such a short space of time was more than three times the population the Maori had reached after 500 years. The self-generation of this new population meant that the total reached its first million by 1908.

It was inevitable that eruptions would occur at the fault line where the pressure of the new capitalist culture of imperial Britain began to overwhelm an ancient, indigenous culture that had already been weakened by the invading forces of the previous 40 years. The wars that broke out between Maori and settlers in the 1860s were fought principally in Taranaki, the Waikato, Bay of Plenty and East Coast regions, not surprisingly across some of the most fertile and desirable land in the North Island. Because Britain remained responsible for New Zealand's defence and foreign affairs, the local government was able to call on imperial troops as well as its own militia. And the battle lines were never clear-cut, often complicated by tribal rivalries that saw some Maori fighting on the settler side.

The ability of Maori warriors to resist and counter the superior numbers and weaponry of Pakeha soldiers had already been demonstrated during Governor George Grey's tussles with Hone Heke and Kawiti during the Northland wars of the mid-1840s. But British commanders continued to underestimate Maori prowess and tactics. Maori knew they could not beat British forces on an open battlefield, facing cannon barrage and then disciplined musket fire followed by bayonet charges. They adapted their fortified pa to withstand cannon fire and dug trenches for individual protection. Add secret tactical withdrawal, outflanking movements and ambush, and Maori made a formidable adversary; on occasions, such as at Gate Pa (Tauranga) and during

Titokowaru's advance on Wanganui, they inflicted telling defeats. Maori warriors had to wage war part-time while they continued to till and harvest gardens, forest and sea so that their whanau could survive. For a time in the Waikato, hapu and iwi co-operated, rotating responsibility for providing warriors for the battlefield, but lacked the kind of logistical infrastructure that was able to sustain British professionals in the field. Eventually, numbers of both men and guns, and military professionalism, overcame Maori resistance. At the peak of the wars 18,000 British soldiers were employed, roughly equivalent to the total population of able-bodied Maori men.

The final victory of British and settler forces over Maori by 1872 almost brought about the destruction of the entire race. Vast areas of land were confiscated in Taranaki, Waikato, Bay of Plenty and Hawke's Bay, and went on to be cleared and settled by Pakeha farmers. While Maori resistance to white settlement and culture lingered on into the new century in such bush and mountain strongholds as the Urewera and King Country, Maori hold on their land had been fatally loosened, their mana and morale severely weakened. The Treaty became a 'nullity' and land law was administered in favour of farming settlement and development. On the eve of the wars Maori population had still been nearly half New Zealand's total (56,000 compared with the Pakeha 60,000). By 1886 Maori had sunk to below 10 per cent of the total, and at the turn of the century their numbers dipped below 40,000. They had become a small minority in their own land and Dumont d'Urville's predicted Europeanisation had been completed.

During the period of the wars Auckland continued to flourish as the capital (until 1864, when the seat of government shifted to Wellington) and as the northern maritime and trading centre for timber, kauri gum and Coromandel gold. It was also the headquarters for the British armies operating down the military road into the Waikato. The rest of the North Island languished economically under the disruption of the wars and the difficulties posed for forest clearance and communications by the steep and contorted hill country of the interior.

By virtue of an insignificant Maori population, plains and downlands ideal for sheep farming and the discoveries of rich gold deposits, the South Island became the economic powerhouse of the nation for half a century from the late 1850s. Within a decade two-thirds of New Zealand's population lived in the South Island, and the North could not claim a majority again until the end of the century. Already, in 1861, South Island pastoralists shepherded more than two million sheep, nearly 80 per cent of the national total. In that same year gold strikes in Central Otago brought about the rapid enrichment and growth of Dunedin and the Otago settlement. It became the premier financial centre, its banks and insurance institutions bankrolling development throughout the country. Wealth from the sheep stations of Canterbury and gold from the West Coast rushes also saw Christchurch become a leading market capital. If gold completed Dunedin's Presbyterian First Church in 1873, wool propped up Christchurch Cathedral's Anglican spire in 1881.

The momentum of profits from sheep and gold saw the rapid development of a road and rail network in the South Island and then across the North in a continuing development boom that

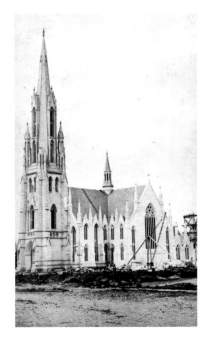

TOP: *Droving sheep: Mount Alford Station on the Canterbury Plains near Mount Hutt in the 1870s. Canterbury province rode into the future on the sheep's back. Wealth from wool built great estates, grand country houses and a road and rail network across the plains. (C. Barraud)*

ABOVE: *Wealth from gold saw Dunedin's elegant First Church completed by 1873. (J. Allen)*

ABOVE: *Start of a bush burn at Puketora, East Coast, about 1910. Summer and autumn skies above the North Island were frequently overcast with smoke during the 50 years from 1870 as the wholesale clearance of plain and hill forests for farming took place.*

RIGHT: *Before burning, mature timber trees were cleared from the forest. The most valuable was kauri whose trunks were 'driven' down creeks and rivers to shipping locations at the coast, here at Coroglen, Coromandel Peninsula.*

was fuelled by Julius Vogel's public works programmes and immigration schemes, funded by massive London loans. Over the decade to 1880, new roads and bridges were constructed throughout the country, 2000 kilometres of new railway line were laid and 5000 kilometres of telegraph lines erected; 140,000 new immigrants arrived, two-thirds of them government-assisted. The biggest impact was in the North Island as new land was opened up in previously inaccessible regions.

Wool and gold, and later wheat, were the main exports, 70 per cent to Britain, 20 per cent to Australia. Imports came in similar proportions, if in more infinite variety, in the continuing nexus of imperial trade. It was a pattern that was to remain essentially unchanged for a century until Britain joined the European Community in 1972. New Zealanders had become more British than the British or, as novelist Anthony Trollope put it during a visit in 1873:

> *The New Zealander among John Bulls is the most John Bullish . . . he is more English than any Englishman at home. He tells you he has the same climate,– only somewhat improved; that he grows the same produce,– only with somewhat heavier crops,– that he has the same beautiful scenery,– only somewhat grander in scale and more diversified . . .*

Although some Irish, Germans and Scandinavians had come, New Zealand's population was overwhelmingly British. In their names, the colony's premier cities proclaimed 'Britain of the South Seas' – Wellington, Nelson, New Plymouth, Christchurch, Dunedin, Napier and Auckland. Maori names hung on in the North Island but had become scarce in the South. The country was under new ownership.

ABOVE: *Almost too late, New Zealanders became aware of the need to save the indigenous fauna and flora that remained after the mass destruction of the forests. This poster from 1923 announced the formation of the New Zealand Native Bird Protection Society, forerunner of today's Royal Forest and Bird Protection Society.*

By the later nineteenth century the South Island had become the setting for great estates run by gentlemen sheep farmers, with few smallholdings. In the North, the difficult newly cleared country was more the preserve of family farms hacked out of the bush by new immigrants. In 1867 Wellington farmer William Golder had romanticised such settlers as 'come to divest Nature of those solitary weeds in which she has long been arrayed, in order to deck her with the garb of art', these men showing a 'courage and energy' worthy of the 'exploits of Knights errant'. Thirty years later, William Pember Reeves lamented 'The Passing of the Forest' to axe and fire in the vast clearances:

> *The blackened forest ruined in a night,*
> *The sylvan Parthenon that God will plan*
> *But builds not twice. Ah, bitter price to pay*
> *For Man's dominion – beauty swept away!*

There had been moderate change to the landscape in the 20 years following the Treaty of Waitangi, as the still small Pakeha population was largely confined to the new coastal settlements. But following the wars, and spurred by Vogel's schemes, the landscape was torn apart. In the 50 years until the early 1920s almost all lowland forests, except in inaccessible regions such as South Westland, were felled or burned for alienation to farmland. Between 1840 and the present, native forest cover of all types has reduced from more than 60 per cent of the land area to less than 20 per cent. There was little thought of conservation or adaptation of European methods of farming to suit a new landscape and new soils. Fell, burn, fence and fertilise. Produce more stock, more wool and meat, export, make money, prosper, become rich. The Judaeo-Christian-capitalist gospel legitimised the harnessing of nature, all the beasts of the field and fowls of the air, to serve the needs of the species made in God's own image, in the country that had now come to be known as God's Own.

LEFT: *North Island hill country was fenced into rough sheep paddocks, the ash-rich soil sown with European grasses. In near-isolation, farmers struggled to survive as initial fertility waned and rains brought flood and slip to land no longer held together by the forest's root and branch. Raurimu, c. 1910.*

ABOVE: *In the early twentieth century, cleared lands in Taranaki were turned into cow paddocks as the dairy export industry gathered momentum.*

RIGHT: *The beginning of the dairy export boom. An early butter factory in the Manawatu with farmers bringing their milk for processing, 1905.*

But there were not enough beasts and fowls in New Zealand to fulfil all the settlers' needs. Domestic animals galore were needed for wool, hides, meat and haulage. Familiar animals from the countryside of 'Home' were needed also, for hunting and as security blankets for the homesick attempting to transport an entire culture. Foxes did not acclimatise, but hares and rabbits did, with a vengeance. Robin redbreasts did not make it, but blackbirds, thrushes and sparrows thrived. Deer galloped off into the receding bush, and Australian possums were released to start a fur industry; they both set about browsing to death the forests that farmers couldn't reach. The rabbits became a pest, chewing up what was left of eastern South Island grasslands already burned and then masticated by sheep. Stoats and their mustelid mates were brought to fix the rabbits, but they fixed the native birds instead. Under the onslaught of forest removal and predator attack, scores of endemic birds disappeared. It is hard to say whether the uncontrolled clearance of forest or the willy-nilly introduction of exotic animals was the stupidest action perpetrated on the New Zealand landscape in the century of settlement after 1840. But some people, here and in Britain, made a lot of money and the cities grew and industry developed. As the exotic willows and gorse took over, New Zealand even began to look a little more like Old England.

A worldwide economic depression slowed things down in the 1880s, but the first successful shipment of refrigerated sheep meat to London from Otago's Port Chalmers in 1882 marked the beginning of a new export era. No longer would the country's economy be dependent on fluctuating wool prices and the declining production of gold. The frozen meat export industry expanded rapidly, and butter and cheese soon followed. The clearance and development of new dairying lands in Taranaki and the Waikato coincided with the introduction of refrigeration, and the

ABOVE: *Smoke being discharged from the refrigeration plant aboard the* Mataura, *alongside at Port Chalmers in the mid-1880s. The* Mataura *took the second cargo of frozen meat to Britain in 1882, at the beginning of an export trade that soon came to incorporate dairy products and was to earn the bulk of the country's export income.*

LEFT: *In 1893, New Zealand women were the first in the world to gain the right to vote for a national Parliament. But they did not have the right to stand for Parliament, and the National Council of Women was formed in 1896 as a lobby group to represent women's political interests. The right to stand was granted to women in 1919, but few were elected over the next half-century. In 2001, New Zealand's Governor-General, the Chief Justice, the Prime Minister, the Leader of the Opposition and the Attorney-General were all women.*

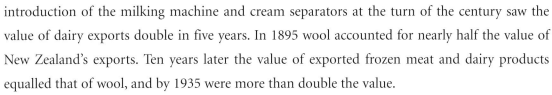

introduction of the milking machine and cream separators at the turn of the century saw the value of dairy exports double in five years. In 1895 wool accounted for nearly half the value of New Zealand's exports. Ten years later the value of exported frozen meat and dairy products equalled that of wool, and by 1935 were more than double the value.

The 1880s depression also brought political change, stirred by the arrival of a universal male franchise and the establishment of the first trade unions. The ideals of egalitarianism, of Jack being as good as his master, had held powerful sway among immigrants from class-ridden England seeking a new life and a new way of ordering society. But by the 1880s, on the great sheepfarming lands of Canterbury, Otago and Hawke's Bay, a landed gentry had developed, aping their ancestors and growing rich off the sheep's back. A high percentage of good land lay under the hand of a few runholders, and there were fewer opportunities for the small farmer to get a start. The plight of the working-class man and land reform issues led to the election of a radical government in 1891 under John Ballance and then 'King' Dick Seddon, who ruled for 13 years before Joseph Ward saw this Liberal administration through to 21 years in office. The great estates were broken up, women were given the vote, old age pensions were introduced and industrial legislation was passed by a reforming government that caused New Zealand to be described as the 'social laboratory of the world'.

All these reforms were enacted during a period when the British Empire reached its zenith and the country enjoyed a period of unprecedented prosperity in the decades before the First World War. New Zealand had become the Empire's farm. Loyalty and affection for 'Home' was at its height. Seddon was quick to send forces to fight on the British side in the South African War.

ABOVE: *Loyalty to Empire saw New Zealand send thousands of soldiers to help Britain fight its enemies in Europe and the Middle East during the First World War. Here New Zealand and Australian troops – Anzacs – land at Gallipoli in April 1915 in an attempt to capture the Dardanelles. The campaign was a disaster and the first sentiments of a separate nationhood were stirred by the appalling loss of more than 2700 dead.*

Continuing the jingoism, Ward announced in 1909 that New Zealand would pay £2 million – a huge sum – to build a battleship for the Royal Navy. New Zealand was quick to answer the call to arms in August 1914 and eagerly invaded German (Western) Samoa as part of the imperial war effort. In April 1915, Kiwi soldiers were sent ashore with Australians, as the 'Anzacs', at Gallipoli in a bungled plan to capture the Dardanelles and bottle up the Turkish fleet. Thousands were slaughtered and maimed in the sequence of mindless fighting that characterised the Great War. In the wasted blood of Gallipoli, New Zealanders first began to realise that being a nation depended on more than unthinking loyalty and sacrifice to Britain's imperial causes. But sentiment, kinship and economic ties kept the new dominion as the child to the dominating mother country. New Zealand did not begin to leave 'Home' for another half-century after the end of the 'war to end all wars'.

New Zealanders, proud of what they had achieved in primary industries and social reforms, were already persistent in asking visitors within a short time of their arrival, 'So what do you think of New Zealand?' There was a tinge of uncertainty in this; the self-conscious teenager seeking approval. English humorist A. P. Herbert in 1925 replied: 'She is beautiful and prosperous and democratic and conservative; she has every virtue and every charm. But why, I wonder, in a country so full of pleasant things, are they so proud of Rotorua?' Writer George Bernard Shaw in 1934

ABOVE: *Prime Minister Michael Joseph Savage inspecting the construction of the New Zealand Centennial Exhibition in December 1938. Nine months later, Savage was the first leader to declare unequivocal support for Britain's declaration of war on Germany. More than 18,000 New Zealanders had died in the First World War; nearly 12,000 were to die in the Second. The country's casualty rate was twice that of Australia's.*

railed at New Zealanders for depending so much on the British market and expecting Britain almost to go to war to make other countries take New Zealand's butter and cheese. New Zealand, he declared, should become self-sufficient.

LEFT: *The Second World War had been preceded by the Great Depression, causing massive unemployment and poverty. Workers across the country protested against the government's economic policies, here on the steps of Parliament in 1932. Relief came with the state intervention policies of Savage's Labour government in 1935. War brought a full employment that was to last for more than 30 years.*

Shaw's prophetic advice was not taken despite the experience of the Great Depression, which saw New Zealand at the mercy of economic misfortune on the other side of the world. The stress and poverty that this caused brought another reforming government to power the year after Shaw's visit. The first Labour government, building on the Liberal heritage and in the spirit of both the United States' New Deal and the Soviet Union's communist reforms, brought the state into people's lives on a scale never before experienced. The 'cradle to grave' welfare state that it built over the next 14 years set standards for state support and assistance in education, health, housing and social security that underpin New Zealand society even today.

New Zealand went to war again with a will in 1939 – 'Where Britain goes, we go', proclaimed Prime Minister Michael Joseph Savage. Again New Zealand forces fought principally on the other side of the world, in the Middle East and Italy. But the Second World War brought the triumph of the American Empire and the beginning of the end for the British Empire, and the consequent cutting of the apron strings to New Zealand. But for 20 years after 1945 the old pattern continued as post-war reconstruction occupied both Britain and New Zealand. Britain took all the food New Zealand could produce, and the years of the Korean War proved a boom for wool, too.

ABOVE: *US servicemen relaxing at a day of waka racing at Ngaruawahia in the Waikato, 1943. While New Zealand troops were fighting 'over there', American troops were 'over here' for training, or rest and recreation, in the Pacific theatre of war. (J. Pascoe)*

RIGHT: *Prime Minister Norman Kirk farewelling the frigate* Otago *as it sets off from Auckland in 1973 with a cabinet minister aboard to protest French nuclear tests in the Pacific.*

Secure in fat profits from primary produce, the welfare state waxed, there was zero unemployment and Kiwis could boast the best standard of living in the world.

The first economic cracks began to show in the late 1960s. It was also a time when New Zealanders had begun to question the country's involvement in other people's wars as the Vietnam debacle reached its height. The year 1972 was a seminal period for New Zealand. Britain at last joined the European Community, restricting New Zealand's access to the British market. Labour Prime Minister Norman Kirk struck blows for New Zealand's independent place in the world by unilaterally recognising Communist China and, later, sending a frigate with a cabinet minister aboard to Mururoa Atoll to protest French nuclear testing in the Pacific. New Zealand was coming of age and finding its own voice.

Economic conditions grew tougher after the oil shocks of the 1970s. But National Prime Minister Robert Muldoon tried to hang on to the New Zealand of the 1950s and 1960s – 'New Zealand the Way You Want It' – by excessive overseas borrowing and economic measures, such as

ABOVE: *Part of the vast wine-growing estates that have been established in Marlborough over the past 20 years. New Zealand wines now have an international reputation as part of the growing diversity of horticultural products being exported to markets around the world.*

LEFT: *'Adventure' tourism has become a key attraction for domestic and international travellers alike. Integral to this is the jetboat, invented by New Zealander Sir William Hamilton in the 1950s, which here rides the rapids below the Huka Falls on the Waikato River near Taupo.*

price controls, that had almost brought the country to its knees by 1984. Inflation and unemployment had both begun to climb. Another reforming Labour government swept into power, not with socialist plans for state intervention and improvement for the workers, but intent on giving everyone a free-market cold bath. Over the next decade New Zealand became the most financially and economically deregulated country in the world. Its free-market experiments were hailed in what had become 'the economic laboratory of the world'. The cold bath cured some dangerous monetary ills and brought about the most diversified economy in the country's history. While primary produce remained paramount, its variety increased beyond earlier imagination – from venison to fine wine – and was sent to almost every market in the world. By the 1990s Britain took just six per cent of New Zealand's exports. Steadily, growing from the 'clean, green' image of New Zealand's natural environment, tourism expanded to become by the twenty-first century the country's single biggest earner of overseas revenue.

But the free-market cold bath also produced the flu of heavy social costs, as New Zealand slid down on all the health, education and social welfare indicators of the Western world; from being in the top five per cent to the bottom 10. And, for the first time since the breakup of the great wool estates a century before, class reappeared as a reality in society, with an elite of new rich and an increasing underclass. The larger part of this underclass was Maori, who figured worst in all the health, education, unemployment and crime statistics. By 1900 it had seemed that all the Pakeha needed do was 'smooth the pillow of the dying Maori race'. But Maori proved more resilient than that and their numbers slowly recovered during the first half of the century. New educated leaders came forward, and the exploits of the Maori Battalion during the Second World War restored old warrior pride. After this war there was a mass migration of Maori away from the

ABOVE: *In the Maori 'renaissance' of the last quarter-century, there has been a strong resurgence of Maori language and culture. These students are performing at the Maori and Pacific Island Secondary Schools Cultural Festival.*

rural districts where they had been mostly domiciled and into the growing cities to meet the demand for labour.

Growing Maori unemployment and other economic stresses in the 1970s then brought to the fore old grievances over the confiscations and other shoddy land deals and racist treatment during the century past. Demands for redress became cogent. The status of the Treaty of Waitangi was restored and, after 1985, it became possible for Maori to have grievances addressed by the Waitangi Tribunal concerning land claims dating as far back as 1840. Since that time some major tribal claims have been settled, others are pending, and in concert with this process there has been increasing Maori political activism and challenges to existing notions of race, culture and sovereignty that impinge on the very heart of the country's constitution. Meeting and settling those challenges is the nation's greatest task for the twenty-first century.

The Maori 'renaissance' over the last quarter of the twentieth century also meant a revival of interest in language and culture, and in particular an explosion in Maori visual arts, music, dance

and theatre. Concurrently during this period of economic and social upheaval – and as New Zealand's population moves from three to four million – there has been an even greater flowering of 'Pakeha' cultural activity, an outpouring of creativity in all the arts.

There have been other great shifts. There has been increasing equality and opportunities for women, epitomised by the first appointment of a woman to the post of Chief Justice and the first election of a woman prime minister, both in 1999, and the second appointment of a woman as Governor-General in 2000; for the first time in New Zealand history women held all three of the most powerful positions in the country. During the last decade Parliament and the electoral system has undergone reform, following the introduction of proportional representation in 1996. The election of Green MPs in 1999 signalled both the beginning of a new parliamentary movement and the political expression of a growing conservation ethic that has steadily replaced the slash-and-burn approach to the New Zealand landscape that prevailed for 150 years after the signing of the Treaty.

ABOVE: *Among young Maori men there has been a revival of interest in traditional skills. The crew of a waka act as escort to Queen Elizabeth II during her visit to Waitangi in 1990 as part of sesquicentennial celebrations.*

ABOVE: *High and still wild: the summit ridges of Tararua Forest Park, north of Wellington, part of New Zealand's special natural heritage.*

The landscape and its remaining special biota are seen now, not as something to be removed or exploited in the cause of replacing them with the forms, species and values of another culture, but as a natural taonga to be protected and preserved as the core of a firming national identity. The historic isolation that produced that taonga has disappeared for good as the forces of corporate globalisation impinge on New Zealand with increasing cultural and physical effect. McDonald's and Coca-Cola can be found on every main street; multi-national corporates patent

indigenous New Zealand plants; new animals arrive not on the westerly winds but in shipping containers and the holds of jumbo jets. In steadily shedding its old British ties and influences, New Zealand, as a small country with a population that is never likely to be much greater than five million, faces a huge challenge to maintain its sovereign, cultural and natural integrity in the turbulent economic and political times that lie ahead.

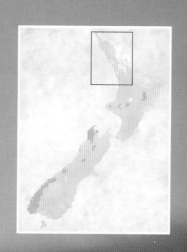

NORTHLAND TO WAIKATO
BETWEEN TWO SEAS

BETWEEN TWO SEAS

THE REGION NORTH of New Zealand's 38th parallel and west of the North Island's dividing ranges has always been a world unto itself. It is a contiguity drawn from geography and climate, a concentration of the richest soils in the country, coasts that yield equally rich harvests, harbours that have seduced settlers with their warmth and shelter, and sun-blinded seaways that have allowed comfortable communication between the top of the Far North's subtropical peninsula and the hot coves of Coromandel.

This is also a place of islands. Any landfall along the region's contorted eastern coastline is first signalled by beacons of peak, cliff or pillar of volcanic islands and reefs. Promising haven in deep bays and tidal inlets and safe anchorage in any conditions, the region has become a yachting paradise of international renown.

In utter contrast, the western coast, from Cape Reinga at the tip of New Zealand down to the black sands of the King Country, is an island-less sweep of endless beaches or cliffs pounded by the ripping surf of the Tasman Sea. This 500-kilometre swing of coast is broached only by half a dozen estuaries guarded by turbulent sand bars, presenting a difficult and dangerous landfall for any ship bearing down on what is most often a lee shore under the prevailing westerlies. These estuaries were once richly fringed with forests of kauri, the great conifer that grows naturally only in this region. And it is a coast that fittingly encompasses the longest continuous beach in the country, Ninety Mile (more nearly, Ninety Kilometre), a belt of high dunes that, bolstered against outcrops of ancient sandstone and limestone, have created a finger peninsula that points the way to the tropics.

PRECEDING PAGES: *Sunrise over Auckland city and the Waitemata Harbour.*

LEFT: *Northland's Bay of Islands, harbour of history and a paradise for yachting and deepsea fishing.*

ABOVE: *Tasman rollers breaking against the rocks of Piha, a favourite surfing and surfcasting beach on the coast west of Auckland city.*

ABOVE: *A sea kayaker glides through the mangroves of the Waitangi River, Bay of Islands. This subtropical tree* (Avicennia resinifera) *graces estuaries as far south as the Bay of Plenty.*

RIGHT: *A pohutukawa* (Metrosideros excelsa), *the 'New Zealand Christmas tree', in flower at Tairua Inlet, Coromandel Peninsula. Occurring naturally along coasts as far south as Taranaki in the west and Poverty Bay in the east, this striking tree has been successfully grown all across the country since European settlement.*

The region has a geological community marked by a confusion of volcanically intruded sedimentary rocks softened by the sandscapes of the western coast and the rich silt and marshlands of the Waikato and Thames river catchments. Most of the region is landmarked by the eroded cones of extinct volcanoes, 63 in the greater Auckland area alone, and these – plus the rise of sea levels and the creation of estuaries through the working of tides and rivers – have created the dissected and irregular landscapes of today. According to geological averages, another volcano is due to erupt within the next 200 years, and if sea levels do rise more over the next century, as warned, then the landscape will change unpredictably again.

The kauri grew naturally north of the 38th parallel, partly because the climate is almost frost-free and produces copious rainfall, but also because this ancient species survived in the only forested region extant during the height of the last ice age. If kauri was the dominant tree of the mixed softwood–hardwood forests, mangrove (manawa) was, and remains, dominant in the inter-tidal zones of the region. Growing to 15 metres high in the Far North, it is present only as a shrub at its southern limit at Kawhia and Ohiwa (Bay of Plenty) – close again to the key 38th parallel. Mangroves, found elsewhere only in truly tropical or subtropical regions, form some of the world's most biologically rich habitats for wildlife. The other spectacular tree emblematic of this region is the pohutukawa, which clings to coastal cliffs like a gnarled octopus and emblazons the north with crimson flowers at the summer solstice – truly 'New Zealand's Christmas tree'.

When Polynesian settlers arrived about 800 or 900 years ago the entire region was covered in dense forest, predominantly kauri and hardwoods in the north and Coromandel, with podocarp–hardwood forests more predominant in the south. Mangroves succoured the estuarine coasts, there were vast swamps in the Waikato and Thames basins, and great dunelands sprawled along Ninety Mile Beach and the Kaipara coast. In such a rich, warm forest environment, birdlife was prolific, including the smaller species of bush moa; the beaches and rocks were alive with

abundant shellfish, the seas teeming with fish. The latest volcano had ceased its steaming, and for gaunt Polynesian voyagers, who had spent weeks at sea in their escape from overpopulated and hungry home islands, this area of Aotearoa must have seemed a paradise.

Legend has it that the exploring navigator Kupe made first landfall in Northland's Doubtless Bay and left again for his homeland from western Hokianga. Maori tradition then tells us that the Te Aupouri, Rarawa and Nga Puhi iwi, who came to populate most of Northland, were descended from East Polynesian settlers who came in the *Mamari* and *Kurahaupo* waka (canoes), which were wrecked on the west and east coasts respectively in the fourteenth century. Before that, small numbers of earlier Polynesian wanderers had roamed the warm coasts in a subsistence hunting economy that left little trace of their presence. Ngati Whatua, north of the Tamaki (Auckland) isthmus, look back to ancestors from the *Mahuhu*, which made its final landfall in the Kaipara Harbour. Waikato and Coromandel iwi claim descent from the *Tainui*, which came to rest at Kawhia. Any earlier settlers of the region were either absorbed or destroyed during this later wave of invading settlement, and the warm, rich and variegated lands of the Northland–Auckland–Waikato region came to embrace about 40 per cent of the Maori population. For 500 years this area has proved the most desirable place to live for the bulk of New Zealanders by virtue of its mild climate, its productive soils, forest and sea, and the relatively easy means of travel available by sea, river and, eventually, road.

ABOVE: *Raglan breakers on the rugged and wild west Waikato coast attract all surfers serious about riding the wave.*

ABOVE: *Maori waka meet a British trading ship in Whangarei Harbour. Northland harbours saw the greatest level of contact between white traders, whalers and missionaries and Maori in the years before the signing of the Treaty of Waitangi in 1840. (C. Heaphy)*

Struggles to control such favoured lands were a continuing source of conflict, but before the arrival of the Pakeha, war had its season, when time could be spared from gardens and kainga, and was driven mostly by utu. These engagements usually involved just a few hundred warriors, but one of the last great traditional battles to be fought with patu (club) and taiaha (wooden staff) was said to have been fought by as many as 9000, near Te Awamutu in 1807. Within a decade muskets arrived, and in 1822 Nga Puhi came down on the Tamaki and Waikato tribes with the new Pakeha weapon and slaughtered or enslaved thousands. A plaque near Pirongia commemorates the place where 'musket overcame taiaha'. Waikato warriors soon retaliated, but injuries still linger in ancestral memory from the time when there were the endless retributions of utu in the pursuit of tribal mana.

Although the northern region was not the first landfall for European discoverers Tasman and Cook, both sailed its coasts and Cook made shore at Mercury Bay (Coromandel), in the estuary of the Thames (Waihou) and at the Bay of Islands, all of which he named. Northland and Coromandel were the two places where, apart from sealing and whaling settlements in the Deep South, the greatest level of interaction before 1840 took place between the new European interlopers and the tribal world of the Maori. The Bay of Islands was favourite port for European and American ships trading and whaling in the Pacific. As Cook reported, it had good anchorages and 'every kind of refreshments', which came to include the alcoholic swill of grog shops.

Beyond the frontiers of British governance, the Bay of Islands also became a refuge for every kind of escapee from the rule of law. When Charles Darwin visited the area aboard the *Beagle* in 1835, he saw it populated by the 'very refuse of society'. The dense Maori population of the bay attracted Christian missionaries, who held the first service at Rangihoua at Christmas 1814. But 20 years were to pass before Maori began to convert in numbers to the white man's God.

The first and principal trade between Maori and Pakeha was in kauri and flax for ship's timber and ropes; one tradition has it that some Royal Navy ships at Trafalgar in 1805 carried kauri spars. Hokianga and the Coromandel were the chief focus of the trade, and by the time of the signing of the Treaty at Waitangi in the Bay of Islands on 6 February 1840, the useful trees of these regions had been cleared well back from their shores. The forests were still vast away from the coast, but the impact of centuries of Maori settlement meant that much of the widespread environs of the most favoured areas, such as Bay of Islands and Tamaki, had been reduced to scrub and fernland through clearance and intensive gardening. The musket wars meant that the once densely populated region of Tamaki–Kaipara was almost deserted.

The Bay of Islands remained a centre of Maori–Pakeha interaction after the Treaty signing as New Zealand's first governor, William Hobson, maintained a year-long makeshift capital there, and again later, in 1845, when it was the focus of the first militant challenge to British authority. Hone Heke four times felled the British flagstaff and, in the brief 'War of the North' that followed, English forces under the direction of Governor George Grey were stretched to put down this 'rebellion'. Following this, Northland lost pre-eminence in national affairs as the focus of politics and power shifted south to the new Pakeha settlements. For the next 70 years the region was famous only for the resources of its great kauri forests as, first, the massive trees were felled to build the new Pakeha towns and, later, kauri gum – tapped from trees or dug as fossilised remnants – became a valuable commodity in the manufacture of linoleum flooring and varnish. Much of the old forested landscape was devastated by felling, burning and gum digging,

ABOVE: *Nga Puhi chief Hone Heke felling the British flagstaff at Kororareka in defiance of British authority. (A. McCormick)*

LEFT: *The settlement of Kororareka (Russell) sketched on the morning of 10 March 1845, the day before Hone Heke felled the flagstaff for the fourth time and destroyed much of the town. It was the beginning of brief war in the north and the end of Kororareka's importance as a port of call. (G. Clayton)*

ABOVE: *Gum diggers at Sweetwater in the Far North about 1914. Swamp and scrub lands harboured fossilised kauri forests, a rich source of the gum used in the manufacture of floor coverings and varnishes.*
(Northwood Bros)

and the 'roadless north' became a backwater while farming, industry and population burgeoned in the south.

Early in 1841 Hobson established his new capital of Auckland – named for his old commander Lord Auckland, then Viceroy of India – on the shores of the Tamaki isthmus. The city started with no grand plan and has continued much the same way since, growing like Topsy along the shores of the Waitemata Harbour; around the Tamaki peninsula and estuary; across the isthmus – just a kilometre wide at its narrowest point – to the Manukau Harbour; west to the Waitakere Ranges; south to Otahuhu, Mangere and beyond to the Bombay Hills; via ferry and then bridge north across the Waitemata to Takapuna and the bays of the eastern coast. Auckland was outnumbered by the Wellington settlement in its first years but, by 1846, had moved ahead and, though Dunedin caught up with it during the peak of the southern gold rushes in the late 1860s, the 'Queen City' has continued to be the largest urban area in New Zealand ever since.

The early town prospered from its fertile, easily accessible hinterland and coastal trade, especially from a growing timber industry. As Pakeha population rapidly increased (and the Maori

declined), there was a rising demand for more arable land in the south. But Maori resistance to further land sales hardened; Waikato, Taupo and neighbouring iwi appointed a king who was expected to protect their lands and maintain law and order. The King Movement's challenge to British sovereignty, and the demands of land-hungry Pakeha settlers, led to war by 1863. The entire Pakeha male population of Auckland enlisted in militia, and 10,000 British regular troops arrived to prosecute the policies of the settler government and Governor Grey. Fortified settlements were established to defend the Auckland isthmus, and a military road was pushed south to the Waikato River as a precursor to invasion. Auckland became a gay regimental town with military reviews and balls, regattas and race meetings.

Prior to the war there had been limited Pakeha influence in the Waikato. A trading post had been established at Waikato Heads in 1830, and five years later missionaries were moving up the rivers to establish stations near Te Awamutu and Matamata. But many Waikato Maori held back from signing the Treaty of Waitangi and from selling their land. Between 1840 and 1860, taking advantage of the skills brought by missionaries, the 'wild Wykatto' transformed their rich river valleys into market gardens and wheat farms, and constructed a number of mills on the Waikato River. Maori boatmen plying the river and Manukau Harbour supplied the growing settlement of Auckland with enormous quantities of food. It was a brief golden spell of Maori economic independence within the new world.

Skirmishing began in July 1863. In October, gunboats and 600 militia under General Cameron overcame entrenched Kingite Maori at Meremere, but three weeks later suffered heavy casualties before overcoming the redoubts of Rangiriri further upstream. Cameron's army pushed on slowly, taking the Kingite headquarters of Ngaruawahia without resistance, then

ABOVE TOP: *The beginning of a metropolis: Auckland a few years after its founding. It remained the capital for 24 years. (J. Merrett)*

ABOVE: *Sir George Grey (1812–98). As Governor of New Zealand (1845–53, 1861–68) and Premier (1877–79), Grey was the most powerful political figure in the country's colonial history.*

ABOVE: *In February 1864, during the Waikato war, British troops outflanked Maori strongholds in a silent night march and surprised the strategically important pa of Rangiaowhia. This scene, drawn from an eyewitness account, shows the death of General Nixon. Maori civilian casualties led to accusations of a massacre. (J. Wilson)*

advanced up the Waipa Valley. In skirting the strong Maori position at Paterangi, the soldiers fell upon the defenceless village of Rangiaowhia, where old men, women and children were killed in an alleged massacre that was to lead to reprisal raids on Pakeha settlers in later years.

The campaign came to its conclusion in April 1864, not far south of Rangiaowhia, when Cameron's 2000 troops assailed 300 defenders at Rewi Maniapoto's redoubt of Orakau. For three days, thirsty and starving, the beseiged Maori held out against the vastly superior force. When General Cameron asked for surrender, Rewi replied with a defiant cry that has echoed down the years as a symbol of all Maori resistance to Pakeha invasion: 'Kaore e mau te rongo, ake, ake!' (Peace shall never be made, never, never!) An offer of safe passage for women and children was equally rejected. The battle finally lost, the Maori defenders charged and burst through the British lines, many escaping south into the wild hills of what became known as the King Country, a centre for continuing resistance over the next 30 years.

Despite the efforts of valiant warriors in the face of overwhelming odds, Maori control of the Waikato had gone forever. In a savage retribution for their resistance, the government confiscated all those Waikato lands as far south as Te Awamutu already unpurchased, and much of the country was divided into 20-hectare settlements and awarded to Pakeha soldiers who had fought in the wars. To begin with, the soldier settlements clustered around military redoubts while fear

of further warfare lingered. Even after reconciliation, led by Rewi Maniapoto in the late 1860s, the region did not prosper, and then suffered badly from the worldwide economic depression of the 1880s. The population of the largest town, Hamilton, sank to only 600, the size of a large village.

While the Waikato languished after the Land Wars, nearby Coromandel boomed with a series of gold rushes that began in 1866. Briefly, with a population of 18,000, Thames rivalled Auckland in size. Prospectors probed every nook and cranny of the jumped-up volcanic ranges, then, when the limited amount of alluvial gold was worked out, turned to quartz mining. By 1871 there were more than 70 mines around Thames, yielding more than £1 million of gold annually, and the reverberation of stamping batteries echoed from the hills until the 1920s. Mines opened later south and east in the Karangahake Gorge and at Waihi, which reached its peak of production in 1909 and continued until the 1950s. Waihi's Martha Mine produced £180 million of gold and silver in 66 years and ranked among the richest in the world. It was also the site for a notorious strike in 1912, the first real test of strength between a rising labour movement and employers and government. The mine was closed for months before a police raid left one striker dead and militant miners were driven out of town.

In 1905 Waihi was three times the size of Hamilton, but by then the economic fortunes of the Waikato had begun to turn. The draining of swamplands, in the Thames region especially, opened up large areas for dairy farming, which could now meet a rapidly growing export market with the widening use of automatic milking machines and cream separators. An improving road

ABOVE: *Union Beach Mine, Coromandel, in the 1880s. The Coromandel region was the North Island's chief goldfield, its mines continuing production until the 1950s.*

network enabled the swift delivery of cream to local dairy factories and the Main Trunk railway line provided bulk transport of butter and cheese and other dairy products to the port of Auckland and refrigerated ships sailing to the markets of Australia and Britain.

After the First World War, as gold and silver mining in the Coromandel faded, the Waikato rapidly overtook Taranaki in dairy production, boasting half the country's population of dairy cows, and the South Auckland–Waikato–Thames Valley region began to thrive as the market garden and 'Dairy Bowl' of New Zealand. It was soon to become famous also for the breeding of the finest racehorses. Inexorably, every last patch of swamp was drained, bush and scrub were cleared until the landscape was transformed into a multitude of cow paddocks, bright green from fertilisers, neatly fenced and shelter-belted with macrocarpa and pine; milking sheds, square, herringboned or circular, scattered over the fields like giant corrugated mushrooms. Natural forest survived only in inaccessible gullies or on scenic-reserved hills that crouched on the horizon like dark ancestral memories.

Hamilton, capital of the province, achieved city status in 1945 when its population reached 20,000. By 1975 that had quadrupled, and by 1985, with 140,000 people, the 'River City' had become the fourth-largest in New Zealand. By the 1950s the Waikato was a prime source of electricity for both local and Auckland industries, with hydro dams on New Zealand's longest river and thermal

LEFT: *Matamata farmlands in the Waikato. This became prime dairy country following the mechanisation of the dairy industry at the beginning of the twentieth century.*

stations burning Huntly coal. This energy, together with west coast ironsands, also fed New Zealand's only steel mill, at Glenbrook, built in 1969 on the southernmost arm of the Manukau Harbour. Land confiscation and social exclusion meant that only a few Maori were able to share in Waikato's burgeoning economic affluence. Some 150 years after the signing of the Treaty of Waitangi, the settlement awarded to Tainui, making retribution for lands taken away in the 1860s, began supplying resources for Waikato Maori to guide their own economic future. The King Movement, symbolically, has survived and Ngaruawahia remains the marae of the Maori Queen.

The Coromandel experienced a kauri rush in the exploitation of its forests in the early nineteenth century, followed by a gold and silver rush that, when it passed, left the peninsula racked and ruined. Like Northland, it became a backwater of dusty winding roads and tiny coastal settlements. However, as road access from Auckland quickened to just two hours' drive and the city's population increased, the Coromandel became an increasingly favoured holiday destination, encompassing the brilliance of sand, sea and sun against the dark stillness of hills now in reserves to encourage the slow recuperation of kauri bush in the new age of conservation.

The bays, harbours and beaches of Northland have also become a recreational Mecca for people escaping the metropolis astride the Tamaki isthmus. Until the Second World War, access to the north from Auckland was principally by coaster, but road development has brought its only

The sand, sea and sun of the northern coasts.

ABOVE: *Cathedral Cove, near Hahei, Coromandel Peninsula.*

RIGHT: *Ocean Beach near Whangarei Heads, Northland.*

city, Whangarei (population 45,000 and 175 kilometres distant) within three hours' drive. The port of Whangarei is the export outlet for the farming and horticultural produce of the region, and its harbour hosts New Zealand's only oil refinery, at Marsden Point.

In many ways Northland remains a backwater economically, where pockets of good farmland lie among scrubby hills that stand in rough testimony to the devastation of the kauri forests before the First World War. But the great kauri comes again and there are signs of regeneration everywhere, naturally or from replanting. And some morsels remain of the original forests, most notably Waipoua on the north-west coast, where New Zealand's oldest and greatest trees stand: Te Matua Ngahere (Father of the Forest) is 2000 years old, and Tane Mahuta (God of the Forest) stands more than 51 metres high with a girth of 14 metres and an estimated timber content of 245 cubic metres.

Sandy bays and inlets characterise Northland's eastern coast, providing fabulous cruising grounds. The largest, the Bay of Islands, attracts most yachting visitors for its variety of anchorages among the 150 islands, its deepsea fishing and its historical associations going back for almost two centuries. The Kerikeri Mission House, built in 1822, is the oldest European building in New Zealand. The bay's western counterpart, just 30 kilometres over the hills, is the Hokianga Harbour, steeped also in history both Maori and Pakeha, but darker and more brooding with its estuarine mangroves and scattered villages that speak of decay and distance. The Bay of Islands is bright and rich, decorated by groves of oranges and lemons, a lodestone for tourists. The Hokianga reminds us of the hurt land, a place of spirits that cannot be souvenired.

Nor can the Far North's Aupouri Peninsula, like one great ocean dune between the Tasman Sea and the South Pacific, at its base only five kilometres wide. It is possible to drive almost the entire length of the peninsula along Ninety Mile Beach to arrive at the top of New Zealand at Cape Reinga. This is not just a journey to the end of the road and New Zealand's northernmost

LEFT: *Downtown Auckland. The Force Entertainment Centre on the edge of Aotea Square has it all in terms of old and new: it features an IMAX cinema, the restored 1920s Civic cinema, plus restaurants, bars and shops.*

lighthouse; you will have followed the way of the spirits of Maori dead who journey north towards their mythical homeland of Hawaiiki. At the last stream before reaching Reinga, spirits may choose to take a last drink of mortality. Those that decline return to their recovering mortal coil; those that drink go on, to the pohutukawa tree that twists from the cape's cliffs (and is reputedly 800 years old) in order to descend its roots to the underworld.

Auckland today covers hundreds of square kilometres and continues to grow north, south, east and west. Its population is over a million and climbing, small by world standards but huge by New Zealand's when the next largest urban areas – Greater Wellington and Greater Christchurch – do not reach a third of that total. Auckland has always had the air of a frontier town, a place to try out, to speculate, to buy up, to boom and go bust. Its sprawling, loose and slightly flashy character, with little sense of history or of the need for one, has always marked it as a place apart from other New Zealand conurbations, whose growth has been guided by some sense of what a city or society should be. If Auckland has a sister in character and situation, it is Sydney, another sprawl of suburbs in search of a city; but Auckland is smaller, more temperate, more physically enchanting, reclined between two sparkling seas, its graceful icon of Rangitoto Island figured against the rising sun.

Auckland is the commercial and industrial capital of the country, feeding from its own self-generating market and exporting much of its manufacturing wealth and the produce of the rich South Auckland–Waikato hinterland. It is the country's media and entertainment centre, with

RIGHT: *Samoan dancers celebrate their contribution to the status of Auckland as the capital of Polynesia.*

FAR RIGHT: *The City of Sails. Weekend yacht racing over the waters between North Head, Devonport and Rangitoto Island to the east. On Auckland's Anniversary Day each January, the biggest one-day regatta in the world celebrates the city's founding.*

New Zealand's principal television channels based in the city, as are almost all of the country's national magazines, newspapers and book publishers. The business and industrial activity generated in Auckland and its pleasant climate and glittering situation attract migrants from all over New Zealand – in the infamous 'drift north' – and from overseas, especially the Pacific and Asia. Auckland has strong Samoan, Tongan and Cook Island communities, which, with its high Maori population, make it the Polynesian capital of the world. Over the last 20 years there has been increasing migration from East Asia, too, contributing to a vibrant cosmopolitan atmosphere common to all Pacific Rim cities.

The recreational glory of Auckland is its yachting waters – the Waitemata Harbour and Hauraki Gulf, west to the Coromandel and north to the horizon islands of Great Barrier and Little Barrier, the latter a restricted sanctuary for birds such as kakapo, kokako, saddleback and stitchbird now lost to the mainland of New Zealand. Every weekend – every day it seems – the waters are thronged with sails or the stately piles of gin palaces for the less active and adventurous. Sailing and the sea are in the blood here, and Auckland has produced the best yachts and sailors in the world. Sir Peter Blake and Grant Dalton have broken round-the-world and transoceanic records under sail; others have taken world trophies in every racing class and have gone out to win and keep the premier trophy of world yachting, the America's Cup. Every year, at the end of January on Auckland's Anniversary Day, the harbour and gulf are thronged by thousands of craft in the biggest one-day regatta in the world, all celebrating Auckland's true sobriquet as the 'City of Sails'.

TARANAKI & KING COUNTRY
'ASK THAT MOUNTAIN'

'ASK THAT MOUNTAIN'

ON A GREAT CAPE projecting from the western coast of the North Island stands the snowy beacon of Taranaki/Mount Egmont (2518 metres). Visible across the ocean from as far away as the top of the South Island, it was described by Captain Cook as 'of a prodigious height', while his botanist Joseph Banks considered it 'certainly the noblest hill I have ever seen'. Perhaps second only to Milford Sound or Aoraki/Mount Cook, Taranaki became an instantly recognisable icon of natural New Zealand, embodying mountain, volcano, luxuriant bush and fertile surrounding plains. Maori on its southern flank believe 'Taranaki is the mountain, Taranaki is the tribe and Kurahaupo is the canoe' of their migration. It could now be said that Taranaki is also the province. And both province and mountain are guarded in the north by the angry contorted hills of the dark King Country, and in the south by the great moat of the Whanganui River.

Taranaki scoured out the bed of the Whanganui after he lost his mythic battle with Tongariro for the hand of Pihanga (see page 83) and was led to the western edge of the land by his female guide To Toka a Rauhotu. They fell asleep when they reached the coast of the setting sun, only to wake and find that nearby Pouakai had bound Taranaki fast with an arm of land. Only To Toka can release him from bondage, and for uncounted centuries she has remained silent, carved in the rock at Puniho Pa. Jealously she watches Taranaki as he weeps for his lost Pihanga in cloud and rain, or rages in winter gales at his old rivals Tongariro and Ngauruhoe, who answer in angry plumes of smoke and fire. To show Pihanga that he is still chief and will one day return to claim her, Taranaki often displays his cloak of kaka feathers – clouds and snow in sunset light.

PRECEDING PAGES AND ABOVE: *Taranaki/Mount Egmont (2518 metres) from the north-western Pouakai Range.*

LEFT: *Taranaki black ironsands at the Mokau River mouth, where the Tainui waka reputedly landed, casting its anchorstone overboard to remain for many generations to come.*

ABOVE: *A scouting party of Forest Rangers above the Whanganui River in 1865. The painter of this scene, Major Gustavus Von Tempsky, was a Prussian military officer famous for his daring exploits during Land War campaigns in the Waikato and Taranaki.*

Maori who settled the southern slopes of the mountain claim that the first man to climb it was their ancestor Tahurangi, sometime in the fourteenth century, after he came ashore from the *Kurahaupo*. He kindled a fire on the summit to proclaim his tribe's right of ownership, transcending the rights of the first people who had settled the land. Thereafter the upper slopes of the mountain were tapu, though the Taranaki people travelled its forests in search of birds and penetrated its valley heads to collect kokowai – the valuable iron ochre used to produce a red paint pigment.

This whole region – the King Country, Taranaki and Whanganui watershed – was covered in dense forest (except for high mountain tops), unmodified other than from natural damage caused by the eruptions of Taranaki. The western cape of the North Island was formed by volcanic activity, beginning nearly two million years ago. The Sugarloaf Islands, offshore from the present city of New Plymouth, and the onshore spire of Paritutu are the extruded plugs of the first volcano. The next volcano was Kaitake, about 15 kilometres to the south, active about 575,000 years ago, followed by Pouakai, 240,000 years ago – all before Taranaki itself began erupting about 70,000 years ago. The volcano's existing cone began to form 20,000 years ago, and lava flows continued from it, and subsidiary Fanthams Peak, until about 3,300 years ago. Explosive eruptions of ash and pumice occurred as recently as about 1750, destroying both forest and Maori settlements on the higher slopes. Dormant since, Taranaki may slowly erode away like its more ancient neighbours, erupt again, or an entirely new volcano may form along the ancient line of volcanic progression.

After the fourteenth century the Taranaki iwi established its boundaries in collision with tribes of the Ati Awa confederation to the north, and in the south with Ngati Ruanui. Almost all the mountain came under Taranaki control with pa and kainga established as high as 600 metres. The King Country to the north became the preserve of Ngati Maniapoto, and the Whanganui Valley the home of Te Ati Hau. The river marked the southernmost boundary of what came to be called Iwitini – that favoured area of the North Island which, incorporating Taranaki, King Country, Waikato, Coromandel, the coastal zones of Bay of Plenty, East Cape and Hawke's Bay and the whole of Auckland/North Auckland, included about three-quarters of Maori population.

The first sign that the Taranaki world had begun to change forever came in 1818, when Ngati Toa fighting chief Te Rauparaha made the first of his raids south and won battles with the aid of two muskets, the first to be seen in the region. Worse was to follow when heavily armed Waikato came south in 1826 and cornered many of the Taranaki tribe in a pa high on the western slopes of the mountain. A survivor lamented, 'What could Maori weapons do against muskets? The guns did their work so effectually that our people were gathered up as crops of potatoes.'

By the end of the 1830s most of the Ati Awa and Taranaki peoples had been killed, taken into slavery or had fled south. When the New Zealand Company ship *Tory* anchored off the Sugarloaf Islands at the end of 1839, no more than 200 Maori were scattered across the Taranaki district.

The land for a new British colony seemed there for the taking. The Company's naturalist Dr Ernst Dieffenbach went ashore and, with whaler James Heberley, made the first recorded ascent of Taranaki, then known by Cook's title of Mount Egmont (after a First Lord of the Admiralty). Dieffenbach made a useful scientific survey of the area west of the summit to the coast, found traces of oil, and reported that 'the whole district of Taranaki . . . rivals any in the world in fertility, beauty, and fitness for becoming the dwelling place of civilised European communities'.

The first shiploads of British settlers arrived in 1841 and founded the town of New Plymouth. Almost immediately conflict arose over land tenure and purchase as exiled or enslaved Taranaki and Ati Awa people returned to their homelands, following the pacification brought about by the Treaty of Waitangi and increasing conversion to Christianity. Disputes sharpened between Maori and Maori and, most violently, between Maori and Pakeha as the population of white settlers steadily increased.

Conflict over the purchase of Ati Awa land at Waitara led to the declaration of martial law in February 1860 and the start of outright war, a conflagration that quickly spread north to the Waikato, Bay of Plenty and East Coast. European technology and numbers were bound to win a

ABOVE: *The first, and most famous, depiction of Mount Egmont, from the shores of the South Taranaki Bight. Painted at the end of 1840 by New Zealand Company artist Charles Heaphy, and published as a lithograph in London in 1842, this watercolour became emblematic of the romantic vision of New Zealand as a land of fertility and beauty, ideal for British settlement.*

ABOVE: *Missionaries landing at Taranaki, early 1840s. Missionaries often acted as intermediaries and interpreters in conflicts between settlers and Maori. Their pacifying influence in the Whanganui Valley contributed much to the fact that, by 1848, tens of thousands of acres of Maori land had been planted in wheat to feed the new settlements.*

(G. Baxter)

prolonged war, and, when martial law was lifted in July 1865, Maori sovereignty over Taranaki had been effectively destroyed. Much tribal land was confiscated, the last in 1881 following the heroic passive resistance movement of Taranaki chief and prophet Te Whiti o Rongomai at Parihaka.

The destruction of Taranaki mana was completed by Pakeha possession of Mount Egmont and the Pouakai Range. But in 1881, too, the government confirmed all land within a 10-kilometre radius of the summit of Egmont as a reserve to prevent further farming encroachment on a mountain that was also becoming a spiritual icon for many Pakeha. In 1900 it was declared New Zealand's second national park in an ultimate act of protection. Egmont National Park now encompasses nearly 34,000 hectares. In 1978, in an act of reconciliation, the government acceded to a Taranaki Maori petition and returned their sacred mountain so that the iwi might gift it themselves to the people of New Zealand. The proud mountain once again became known as Taranaki.

Similar conflicts over land, initiated by the doubtful 'purchases' of the New Zealand Company, occurred further south at the new town of Wanganui, to the point where it was almost abandoned in 1847. A land settlement the following year allowed security for the development of farms on the rich lands about the mouth of the great river whose source lay nearly 300 kilometres inland on the slopes of Ruapehu. For the dominant iwi, 'Ruapehu is the mountain, Whanganui is the river, Te Ati Hau are the people', and when missionary Richard Taylor first travelled up the densely populated river in 1843 he found a hundred canoes drawn up for a hui at the head of one small tributary.

Cutting deeply through soft papa sandstones and mudstones from the Volcanic Plateau to the sea, the Whanganui had created the only easily navigable route from the west coast to the interior and Lake Taupo. Maori had names for 240 rapids that were milestones over the long journey of 200 kilometres from the tidal limit to inland Taumarunui.

Taylor and other missionaries brought the churches, missions and names of European religion and civilisation that, in Maori translation, figure the river today – Atene (Athens), Koriniti (Corinth), Ranana (London), Hiruharama (Jerusalem). Maori were soon persuaded to abandon their fortified pa at the crests of high papa bluffs and take to agriculture. By 1848 about 30,000 acres of wheat were grown along the lower reaches of the river, and several flour mills were established in the 1850s. Settler demand for more land, as elsewhere, caused war in the valley during the 1860s. Some of the fiercest attacks on British authority were waged by supporters of the Hauhau cult. Their attempts to attack the town of Wanganui and lower river settlements were repulsed in a series of battles, settlers assisted by anti-Hauhau Maori, the last taking place at Pipiriki in 1865.

When hostilities ceased, Te Ati Hau withdrew upstream of Pipiriki, closing their lands off to Europeans. In parallel to Te Whiti's resistance movement at Parihaka, Wanganui chief Kepa Te Rangihiwinui ('Major Kemp') set up a land trust in 1880. Four carved poles marked the boundaries of an enormous area of land, incorporating the Whanganui watershed, within which he stated that no land could be owned by Europeans and which could be administered only by those with ancestral rights. 'If you sell your land you will become slaves,' his followers were told. However, neither Te Rangihiwinui's poles nor Te Whiti's policy of passive resistance could stem the wave of European forest clearance and farm settlement. By the end of the century, ancient Maori traditions of power and population had gone forever.

The broken, gorged and heavily bushed King Country proved the last redoubt for Maori resistance to the European invasion. After their defeat at Orakau in the Waikato in 1864, King Tawhiao and his people withdrew south to Te Kuiti and the edge of 'Aukati', the line that no one can pass, a tapu boundary that marked the edge of all the high country to the north and west of Lake Taupo, as far as the Tasman Sea, and south to the headwaters of the Whanganui and the rim of Taranaki. Here the Kingites were joined by rebels fleeing government retribution, including the

ABOVE: *'A trooper of the Wanganui Cavalry attacked by the Hau-haus' by J. Moultray. During the 1860s Land Wars, the fanatical Maori revivalist cult, Hauhau, spread throughout the North Island. Its followers cast themselves in the role of Israelites (Maori) persecuted by the Egyptians (Pakeha), and Hauhau warriors believed they could not be harmed by bullets.*

ABOVE: *The town of Wanganui in
1888. After early disputes and fatal
conflicts over land purchase in the
1840s, Wanganui grew rapidly as
the port and service centre for the
Whanganui Valley. During the
Land Wars, local Maori helped
defend the town against
Hauhau warriors.*

RIGHT: *After the Land Wars,
prophets Te Whiti o Rongomai and
Tohu led a passive resistance
movement against Pakeha land
settlement in Taranaki. Settler
government soldiers and the Armed
Constabulary ended the 'rebellion'
in November 1881 by occupying the
prophets' pa at Parihaka.*

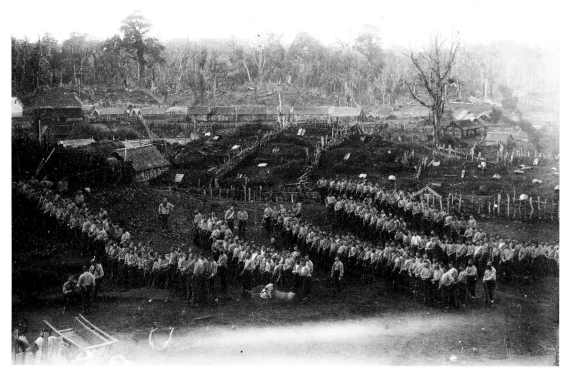

hunted guerrilla leader Te Kooti, and they retreated into the forested interior beyond the Aukati,
beyond the reach of government for 17 years. In 1881, the same year as Te Whiti's arrest and Te
Rangihiwinui's futile boundary poles, Tawhiao left his 'King Country' with 600 followers and, in
a gesture of peace, surrendered a large number of guns to Major William Mair at Pirongia. Mair
gave Tawhiao his own rifle as a gesture of friendship, and the long and intermittent Land Wars
were finally at an end.

During the last decades of the nineteenth century, land surveying, bush felling and establishment of farms throughout Taranaki and Wanganui (and later the King Country) gathered
momentum, greatly aided by the extension of road and rail communications made possible by
the end of Maori resistance to settlement. The cessation of the wars meant that the Main Trunk
railway could be constructed through Te Kuiti to Taumarunui. This became an important transport junction for a burgeoning sawmilling industry, both as a railhead and as the terminus for
steamboats plying up the Whanganui River. The first steamer service from Wanganui to Pipiriki
in 1891 was extended in 1903 to the river's navigable limit at Taumarunui. Steamers provided the
only substantial transport for the people and goods of the river settlements and at the height of
the riverboat service a dozen steam and motor vessels plied the river, the largest a 32-metre stern
wheeler licensed to carry 400 passengers.

Steamer travel up the 'Rhine of New Zealand' rapidly became a major tourist attraction. By 1904 up to 12,000 tourists a year visited the upper Whanganui, many of them continuing on by excursion coach to the Tongariro volcanoes. Much of the surrounding hill country was being developed for sheep farms after the sawmillers had moved through, and many blocks were balloted to returned servicemen in soldier-settlement schemes after the First World War. But during the 1920s and 1930s it became plain that the larger part of the rough and unstable hill country about the Whanganui and in the King Country was unsuitable for agriculture. Farmer after farmer attempted to turn the bush into grassland, employing primitive 'cut and burn' methods. But decreasing soil fertility, erosion, flooding, bush regeneration, falling prices during the Depression and difficult access saw the slow rise and rapid fall of most holdings. The Mangapurua Valley, with its famed 'Bridge to Nowhere', was a typical example of this pattern – the land was cleared, developed and abandoned in one generation between 1917 and 1942.

The Whanganui riverboats flourished until the time of the Depression, when farms were increasingly abandoned and the tourist trade fell away. The construction of the valley road, which reached Pipiriki in 1934, also spelled the doom of the steamers. The last one ceased to operate in 1958, when it was replaced by the world's first commercial jetboat operation.

In contrast to the tough hill country of the King Country and Wanganui, the lush pastures of Taranaki, fertilised by volcanic ash and well watered the year round, proved ideal for dairying as the butter and cheese export industry developed in the first decades of the twentieth century. Railway and highway development to the south, from New Plymouth through Wanganui to the Manawatu and Wellington, provided the export link for production from the greatest concentration of dairy factories in New Zealand. Taranaki became and remained the 'Dairy Province' for most of the twentieth century, until eventually outstripped by the Waikato region. Jersey cows grazing on smooth green paddocks running away to the symmetrical, snow-capped cone of Mount Egmont – New Zealand's 'Mount Fuji' – became a persistent symbol in overseas promotion and was the foundation for the country's 'clean green' image. Despite being 'out on a limb' to the west, Taranaki grew rich on dairy fat and New Plymouth grew from a beleaguered outpost to a prosperous city of 50,000. Dieffenbach's vision of the province as ideally having the 'fertility, beauty and fitness' for settlement was fulfilled.

The settled rustic calm of cow paddock and mountain was disrupted by a new phase in Taranaki's economic life when a natural-gas field was discovered at Kapuni in 1962, and then the vast Maui offshore field seven years later. Taranaki became the 'Energy Province' as its natural gas fired not only thermal power stations and home heaters but was also used to produce urea fertiliser and converted to methanol and gasoline. In the 1980s, onshore exploration discovered economic oil fields east of the mountain between New Plymouth and Stratford that now provide a useful portion of New Zealand's petroleum needs.

Taranaki remains the central plinth to the North Island west coast region. The peak and its

ABOVE: *The limestone papa country of the Whanganui watershed has been worn into tableland, canyon and gorge. The dirty flow of this tributary indicates how clearance for farming upstream has produced erosion and loss of topsoil.*

ABOVE: *The slopes and valleys radiating out from Taranaki/Mount Egmont to the Tasman Sea have been transformed into rich, intensively farmed dairylands.*

park draw in many visitors to walk and climb and ski, and to explore the character of a unique subalpine forest that is no more than an hour's drive from the beaches of the Tasman Sea. Taranaki is the most climbed mountain in New Zealand, and consequently has recorded the highest death and accident toll. Deceptively easy to scale, its heights can become an icy tomb for those caught by the sudden arrival of Tasman storms.

Taranaki is joined now by good highways through the still-incorrigible hills of the King Country to the remarkable attractions of the Waitomo complex of caves. These limestone caverns are pillared by fantastic stalagmites and stalactites and lit by glow-worms that turn them into subterranean yet celestial cathedrals. The road runs swiftly south, too, to the recently created Whanganui National Park. Though steamers have gone and many farms have reverted to bush,

the river is busy again with different kinds of craft – the canoes, rafts and jetboats of fishers, hunters and trampers seeking adventure tourism from the mountains to the sea.

'Ask that mountain,' prophet Te Whiti o Rongomai said in old age. 'Taranaki saw it all.' Saw the coming of the Maori, greeting them with the signals of eruption. Saw the conflicts between them, the first clearing and burning of the forest at its coastal hem. Became still and silent at the sight of the Pakeha settlers and the terrible laying waste of all the forests within view from its highest slopes. Saw the savage conflicts between Maori and Pakeha, the taking of peaceful Te Whiti. Witnessed the farming transformation of all the lands that radiated from the circular margin of its last forests; the flaming banners of energy drawn from the roots of the mountain that came to light the coastal night and the long ocean horizon.

ABOVE: *Winter climbers reach the shelter of Syme Hut on the Fanthams Peak outlier of Taranaki.*

BAY OF PLENTY & VOLCANIC PLATEAU
TRIANGLE OF FIRE

TRIANGLE OF FIRE

THE EXPLOSIVE HEART of New Zealand lies within a fiery volcanic triangle, its base at the Bay of Plenty, its apex at the 2796-metre summit of Ruapehu, the North Island's highest mountain. The triangle of fire lies over an unstable tectonic zone where the Pacific Plate slips deep beneath the Indo–Australian Plate and becomes most active, creating a line of volcanoes that stretches 2000 kilometres across the South Pacific to Tonga.

Maori legend tells that fire and eruption started with a quarrel between god warriors who lorded it over the heights at the centre of the island, now encompassed by Tongariro National Park. Taranaki stood between Tongariro and Ruapehu – where the lakes Nga Puna a Tama now lie – and to the north of Tongariro, Tauhara and Putauaki stood where Lake Rotoaira today reflects the hem of Pihanga. All the warriors sought the hand of soft Pihanga, draped in green forest robes, and their adulation filled the skies with fire, their passion shook the earth. Rivalry grew until there was a great battle and for many days and nights the giants raged, spewing forth lava and exploding rock until there remained a sole victor – Tongariro.

The defeated warrior volcanoes had to escape the battleground under the cover of a single night. When the sun rose after the cataclysmic battle, Taranaki had reached the coast of the setting sun, scouring out the bed of the Whanganui River on his way west. Putauaki fled northeast to Kawerau, close by the Bay of Plenty. But Tauhara dragged his feet, casting disconsolate glances behind at his lost Pihanga, and remained forever where he might see her from the farther shore of Lake Taupo.

PRECEDING PAGES: *Mount Ngauruhoe (2291 metres) in winter, looking west to Taranaki in the distance.*

LEFT: *The view from Ngauruhoe, looking south over the Tama Lakes to Ruapehu, at 2796 metres the North Island's highest mountain.*

ABOVE: *White Island or Whakaari, New Zealand's most active volcano, 50 kilometres off the coast of the Bay of Plenty, erupting from the Pacific's 'ring of fire'.*

ABOVE: *Pohutu ('Splash') at Whakarewarewa thermal area, Rotorua, is New Zealand's largest geyser, reaching up to 30 metres in height.*

RIGHT: *The fabulous Pink and White Terraces of Lake Rotomahana before June 1886. The enormous silica fans attracted visitors from all over the world. Artists wishing to paint the unique spectacle were charged the handsome sum of £5 by local iwi.*

The geological story tells that the volcanoes, hot springs, geysers and mud pools that so characterise this region – and which are so emblematic of New Zealand in the eyes of the rest of the world – are a mere two million years old. This is a fledgling landscape compared with the 200-million-year-old sedimentary rocks that underlie this volcanism and also form the rugged Kaimanawa Ranges bordering the triangle on the east. So recent and ongoing is volcanic activity that the oldest rocks in Tongariro National Park have been dated at just 261,000 years. The newest are just a few years old, following the last eruption of Ruapehu.

The peaks, cones, craters and lakes within the triangle of fire may each have been formed by a single climactic event, or as a consequence of intermittent activity over a long period of time. The 11 lakes of Rotorua are water-filled vents of eruptions that occurred over the past two million years. The most violent single event within historical time was the explosion that formed Taupo, the country's biggest lake, about 2000 years ago. Ash and pumice from this cataclysmic event covered much of the central North Island and was carried as far north as the Bay of Islands. The forest surrounding the centre of the explosion was buried so quickly by hot ash that it did not burn but was transformed into charcoal. The eruption changed the lower course of the Waikato River and the coloured night skies were observed in Rome. These may have been the Fires of Tamatea, discolouring the Pacific moon in the first signal to Polynesians in the Eastern Pacific that land lay in the south-west corner of the ocean.

The most active volcanoes are White Island, 50 kilometres off the Bay of Plenty coast; Ngauruhoe, formed only 2500 years ago; and older, grizzled Ruapehu. All are capable of eruption

at any time. In quiescent periods the main crater of Ruapehu is filled by a lake. Eruptions expel this, causing mud flows, or lahars, which run down the flanks of the volcano into the neighbouring countryside. A catastrophic outflow of mud and water at Christmas 1953 swept away the railway bridge at Tangiwai, causing the crash of a night express train and the loss of 151 lives.

The Taupo–Rotorua thermal area is replete with the hot-water pools, mud pools, geysers and silica terraces of a continually active volcanic landscape. Many millions of travellers have visited what is the most accessible and varied thermal district in the world – enjoying the hellish, otherworldly atmosphere and the frisson of a sense of imminent eruption. Occasionally the forces of the underworld oblige with shuddering earthquakes or, perhaps once a century, a big blast like the 1886 eruption of Tarawera. The roar of this explosion was heard as far away as Christchurch, the area surrounding the mountain was destroyed, more than 150 people were killed, and volcanic debris was strewn over an area of 16,000 square kilometres. The fabled Pink and White Terraces of Lake Rotomahana were destroyed but the eruption created an entire new set of thermal features. No human hand is needed in the redesign of this landscape. Tread softly for you tread on the earth's thin crust.

ABOVE: *The scene at Rotomahana in the days following the huge Tarawera eruption on 10 June 1886 that destroyed the Pink and White Terraces, buried villages and roads and killed more than 150 people. The roar of the eruption was heard as far away as Auckland and Christchurch.*

The first people to encounter this wild and unpredictable world were Maori colonists from the waka *Te Arawa*, which made landfall at Maketu in the Bay of Plenty. Arawa tribespeople made their home around Maketu and then penetrated inland to the Rotorua lake district. Ngati Awa people settled the wider Whakatane district after landfall there in the *Mataatua*, and groups from Waikato iwi, descendants from voyagers in the *Tainui*, crossed the Kaimais to settle the bay at the foot of the Coromandel Peninsula. It was warm and sheltered country, facing the sun and with pockets of good soils to grow the kumara and other tropical crops the migrants had brought with them. The Arawa people were quick to take advantage of the cooking, heating and bathing opportunities afforded by Rotorua's thermal waters. And they pressed on, exploring into the heartland of the island as far south as the great volcanoes. It is said that while the bow of *Te Arawa* rests at Maketu, the sternpost is the mountain Tongariro.

The greatest Arawa explorer was Ngatoroirangi, navigator of *Te Arawa*. As he travelled south, he stamped his foot in the ground to form hot springs and lakes and, in order to claim and name the land for his people, he climbed Tongariro with his slave, the girl Auruhoe. But he was caught in a snowstorm at the summit, such a strange and terrible experience that he called out to his sacred sisters, distant in the homeland of Hawaiiki, to save him: 'Ka riro au; te tonga! Haria mai he ahi moku!' (I am carried away by the cold south wind – I die from the cold! Send me fire!) He sacrificed his slave to give his prayer more power. And his sisters heard him and persuaded demons of the underworld to send fire beneath the wide ocean, bursting forth at White Island and at Rotorua and Taupo until finally a crater of fire exploded beside Ngatoro, into which he cast the body of Auruhoe. The mountain region became known henceforth as Tongariro – the south wind seized – and the fiery volcano, Ngauruhoe, in memory of the sacrificed slave.

Captain Cook gave the Bay of Plenty its name, in contrast to Poverty Bay, where he had been unable to obtain adequate supplies. Cook never went ashore but the name stuck as appropriate

LEFT: *An early view of Lake Taupo from the south end of the lake, looking towards Mount Tauhara: a replication of the 1841 frontispiece to explorer Ernst Dieffenbach's book* Travels in New Zealand.

to its warm fertility, which, by 1769, already supported a sizeable population. Cook reported seeing 40 or 50 Maori waka and described the country about Whakatane as 'pretty clear of wood and full of plantations and villages'. European encroachment into the region was slight until after the wars of the 1860s, although Tauranga, with its fine harbour, became a busy trading post for the flax industry in the 1830s and both Anglican and Catholic missions were established there. European settlement was deterred by the dangers of tribal wars: in the 1820s Hongi Hika's musket campaigns had extended as far south as the Bay of Plenty and Rotorua, leaving much of the Maketu area deserted for years.

European explorers were much more active in the volcanic region, drawn by its scientific curiosities. In March 1839 Australian botanist John Carne Bidwill climbed Ngauruhoe in defiance of Maori tapu, an action that denied German scientist Ernst Dieffenbach the opportunity to explore Tongariro when he visited the area two years later. However, he was able to explore Taupo, Rotorua and Tauranga, making the first survey of the thermal regions. In mid-1841 Dieffenbach estimated the population of the Rotorua region at 5000.

The Land Wars spilled into the Bay of Plenty in January 1864 when the government sent troops to establish a redoubt at Tauranga in order to prevent reinforcements from the bay reaching King Movement warriors in the Waikato. They were challenged by Rawiri Puhirake, who built a fighting pa close to Tauranga. The British assault on Gate Pa in April 1864 was catastrophic, with 31 soldiers killed and 80 wounded. But the pa was badly damaged and Maori abandoned it to build another. Government forces attacked before the pa and defences were complete, and in this battle 120 Maori were killed for the loss of 10 British dead and 39 wounded. Following this, and the conflict arising from the killing by Maori of Lutheran missionary Carl Volkner at Opotiki, martial law was declared. By the end of 1865 much Bay of Plenty land had been confiscated by the government and given to military settlers. Hauhau rebel Te Kooti raided Whakatane in 1869,

ABOVE: *A photograph from the carte de visite of Tuwharetoa chief Horonuku Te Heuheu Tukino IV. This was taken in the 1880s, about the time Te Heuheu offered the volcanic uplands of Tongariro to the Crown for their protection within what became the world's second national park.*

leaving it in ruins, but Maori sway over the region was effectively at an end.

During the wars the various iwi within the Arawa confederation, centred on Rotorua, had remained loyal to the Crown. But the southernmost iwi, Ngati Tuwharetoa, who claimed direct descent from Ngatoroirangi, had supplied 200 warriors to fight with the Waikato tribes. The saying went, 'Tongariro is the mountain, Taupo is the great sea, Tuwharetoa is the tribe, Te Heuheu is the man.' But after the wars Tuwharetoa lands about Taupo and Tongariro came under threat, first from loyalist neighbouring iwi and then from a government that was progressively surveying and taking over Maori land. To protect sacred Tongariro, chief Te Heuheu Tukino IV offered the volcanoes to the government as a gift, to be preserved for the people of New Zealand in perpetuity. Established finally in 1894, Tongariro National Park was the second in the world after Yellowstone. Beginning with an area of 2600 hectares around the volcanoes, it has since expanded to nearly 80,000 hectares, encompassing almost the entire volcanic upland at the heart of the North Island.

In the absence of trunk roads, travellers to the new national park a century or more ago faced a major expedition. The easiest route was by riverboat up the Whanganui as far as Pipiriki, then by coach over cart roads south of Ruapehu to Waiouru, thence by the Desert Road track to Waihohonu Hut on the southern flank of Ngauruhoe. Access to the area improved with the development of extensive timber milling at the turn of the century and then, above all, by the completion of the Main Trunk railway line from Wellington to Auckland. Outstanding engineering feats were necessary to take the line through the central high country. A series of spectacular viaducts was constructed, together with the famed Raurimu Spiral, which employs a complete circle, three horseshoe curves and two tunnels to carry the line up more than 200 metres in altitude at a gradient of 1-in-50. Trains from the southern and northern sections of the line finally met at Pokaka, just south of the National Park road junction, on 6 November 1908.

The railway brought the national park and its winter playground within reach of the country's two main cities, and visitor numbers increased rapidly after the First World War, with the grand hotel Chateau Tongariro being opened in 1929. The first rope tow was erected in 1938, the start of the North Island ski industry, which today sees tens of thousands of visitors enjoy the Whakapapa, Turoa and Tukino fields on Mount Ruapehu (volcanic eruptions permitting). During the Second World War, New Zealand's major military training camp was established adjacent to the railstop of Waiouru, the high (900 metres) tussock uplands of the Kaimanawa providing ideal country for infantry exercise, artillery shoots and armoured manoeuvres. The National Army Museum stands close by the camp today.

The railway to Rotorua, from Auckland via Hamilton, was also complete by the First World War and greatly inflated the numbers of tourists who visited the thermal region to take the waters. The new spa town of Rotorua had been created in 1881, at Ohinemutu on the shore of Lake Rotorua, and the largest bath house in the Southern Hemisphere was opened there in 1908.

LEFT: *Skiers on the Whakapapa slopes of Mount Ruapehu, the North Island's premier skifield; Ngauruhoe beyond.*

BELOW: *The establishment of the town of Rotorua, on the shore of the lake of the same name, was marked in 1906–07 by the building of a Government Bath House in a style to match the grandiosity of European spas. It contained thermal pools and massage cubicles, and has been redeveloped over the years to incorporate a restaurant, museum and art gallery.*

ABOVE: *Logs extracted from the vast radiata pine forests planted between Rotorua and Taupo provide timber for local building and furniture, and the raw material for a booming export industry in logs, chips, pulp and paper for the Asia–Pacific region.*

RIGHT: *New Zealand's largest lake, Taupo, is fed by the snow waters of the Volcanic Plateau. It is the upland reservoir for the Waikato River and the hydro-electric stations that power the cities of Auckland and Hamilton. The Taupo region is also famous for its trout fisheries.*

Complementing its thermal attractions, Rotorua has grown also as a centre for the promotion and display of Maori art and culture.

By contrast, growth in the Bay of Plenty coastal region was slow, and by the beginning of the twentieth century the European population was only 4000. Dairying later gained a foothold, but agricultural production did not increase significantly until a cobalt deficiency in the soil had been identified and rectified. By 1910 it was recognised that the climate in the Tauranga–Te Puke area favoured a citrus industry and the Bay of Plenty as a whole eventually came to produce a large proportion of New Zealand's subtropical fruits.

A huge expansion of agriculture and industry, and consequently population, took place in the Bay of Plenty during the second half of the twentieth century. During the 1920s the barren pumice lands south of Rotorua had been found ideal for the rapid growth of radiata pine and, progressively, 400,000 hectares of the Kaingaroa Plateau were planted for timber production. This was afforestation on a scale unmatched in New Zealand's history and was the stimulus for exotic forestry development across the whole country. The trees from this region came on stream for harvesting in the 1950s, providing the raw material for huge board and pulp and paper mills at Whakatane, Tokoroa and Kawerau. Later, a lucrative industry developed exporting logs and woodchips to Japan.

The Volcanic Plateau region also boomed with the building of a series of hydro power stations on the Tongariro and upper Waikato Rivers to provide electricity for central North Island cities and the burgeoning metropolis of Auckland. Geothermal energy was also harnessed at the Wairakei power station, the second large-scale geothermal plant in the world. As a consequence

ABOVE: *The 'Chinese gooseberry', originally groomed and marketed from the Bay of Plenty as 'kiwifruit', took the world by storm in the 1960s. The fruit has undergone a recent marketing revival, with the development of a yellow-fleshed variety and a re-branding as 'zespri'.*

LEFT: *Fishermen make their evening cast for trout at Waitahanui on the eastern shore of Lake Taupo.*

of this vast power engineering and timber milling, roading throughout the region was greatly improved. The new town of Turangi was created at the foot of Lake Taupo, and Taupo town boomed as the halfway house on the new and fast State Highway 1 between Wellington and Auckland. The trout fisheries of the lake environs became world-renowned. Taupo grew to be the fly-fishing centre of the North Island and the base for hunting and tramping in the Kaimanawa Ranges and a full gamut of lake water sports.

In the 1960s the orchard belt of Tauranga–Te Puke was found to be ideal for the propagation of a little-known hairy subtropical fruit known as the Chinese gooseberry. Renamed the kiwifruit and groomed to perfection, it took the fruit world by storm, establishing a whole new export industry and copycat developments in California, South Africa and Italy. In the capitals of the world, 'kiwi' became a cuisine garnish rather than the nickname for New Zealanders.

The prime beneficiary of the kiwifruit and timber exporting boom has been the port and city of Tauranga. In 1936 this small town had fewer than 6000 residents. Thirty years later its population had quintupled, and now, with more than 80,000 people, it has become New Zealand's sixth-largest city and is still growing fast. Along with nearby Mount Maunganui on the beach, Tauranga has also become a favourite retirement centre and a holiday destination for surfers, big-game fishermen and tourists en route to the thermal, water and recreational attractions of the volcanic hinterland. It has truly become the Bay of Plenty.

EAST COAST & HAWKE'S BAY
FIRST OF THE SUN

FIRST OF THE SUN

ON ALMOST ANY DAY of the year, when making first landfall from the north-east and the central Pacific, the North Island will appear as Aotearoa, a long white cloud lying across the horizon. As the sailor approaches closer, this will harden as a cloud cap spilling over the Raukumara or Huiarau Ranges trending south-west from East Cape to the central mountains of the North Island. The highest peak in these ranges is Hikurangi (1752 metres), almost certainly named by early Polynesian voyagers for Ikurangi in their native Rarotonga, this 'tip of heaven' marking the end of a long and difficult voyage to a promised land. Today, Hikurangi is sacred to Ngati Porou descendants of settlers from the *Horouta* canoe, and Raukumara commemorates the tradition of their bringing many kumara from Polynesia to plant in the warm soils of the coastal belt.

Sacred landfall for Polynesian voyagers, Hikurangi came to be a symbol of worldwide significance. When the planet was circled with meridians, Hikurangi lay at 178° East of zero at London's Greenwich observatory, just two degrees short of the actual antipodes. Higher than any other point of land close to the antipodes, Hikurangi became technically the first place in the world to see the rising sun. This rational construct for charting and navigation created the myth of a British Empire on which the sun never set, for as it threatened to do so at Tonga or the Tokelaus, close to 180° West, it rose again on Hikurangi. This bright myth of Hikurangi and the east coast being the first places in the world to see the sun was commemorated most recently at the dawn of the new millennium.

PRECEDING PAGES: *Cape Kidnappers, the southern headland of Hawke Bay.*

LEFT: *Mount Hikurangi (1752 metres), near East Cape, is said to be the first place in the world to see the sun rise. It has this happy reputation from being the highest point closest to the 180th meridian east of zero at Greenwich.*

ABOVE: Nothofagus *beech forest on the Kaweka Range west of Hawke's Bay. The Kawekas are part of the sequence of ranges that stretch from East Cape to Wellington, reaching up to 1750 metres and forming the backbone of the North Island.*

ABOVE: *Missionary William Colenso (1811–99) was the first Pakeha to settle in Hawke's Bay (1845) and to explore the central North Island ranges. A man of varied talents, Colenso was also a student of the Maori language and a leading botanist. He was New Zealand's first printer and witnessed the signing of the Treaty of Waitangi.*

The east coast region is almost entirely rugged hill country with the only relative flatlands about the Waipaoa River in the south, which runs into the bay first called Turanganui, and the Waiapu, which runs into the South Pacific just south of East Cape. By contrast, the great bight sweeping south and west of Mahia to the cape of Te Matau a Maui (Maui's Fish-hook) was, when Maori arrived, backed by swamps, plains and wide valleys watered by numerous rivers braiding down from the Ruahine mountains. Its soils were enriched by volcanic ashes that had drifted over the ranges from the great eruptions of the central volcanoes. The entire region was covered in forest, none more luxuriant or mysterious than Urewera, bordering Lake Waikaremoana in the highlands of the Huiarau. Where Ngati Porou came to dominate the rugged eastern cape lands, Ngati Kahungunu occupied most of the eastern coast to their south, with other smaller tribes settling border lands between. But in the Urewera the dominant tribe became Tuhoe, people descended from the *Mataatua* waka, which had made landfall in the Bay of Plenty. Tuhoe – 'Children of the Mist' – and Ngati Kahungunu were in regular conflict over tribal boundaries and the more desirable alluvial lands for growing kumara. And all, including Ngati Porou, were the victims of Hongi Hika's Nga Puhi musket raids of the 1820s.

Captain Cook's first landfall in New Zealand was at Turanganui on 9 October 1769. He renamed it Poverty Bay after a bloody first encounter with Maori and because 'it afforded us no one thing we wanted'. He coasted south from here, observing extensive fires in the forests behind the bight south of Mahia that he named Hawke Bay after Sir Edward Hawke, First Lord of the Admiralty at the time of his voyage. The southern headland of Te Matau a Maui became Cape Kidnappers after an attempt by local Maori to abduct a Tahitian boy from on board the *Endeavour*. Cook reversed his course at Cape Turnagain and, after circumnavigating the North Island via 'Cook's Strait', reached this point once more from the south and proved that New Zealand was probably not the edge of the great southern continent he had been sent to discover.

Europeans were few and far between along the entire eastern coast of the North Island until the 1850s. The Reverend William Williams arrived in Poverty Bay to establish the first mission on the coast in 1840 and was the first Pakeha to travel overland through the Urewera. This journey was repeated the following year by missionary printer and evangelist William Colenso, who met the Catholic Father Claude Baty on the wind-wild shores of Waikaremoana, where they gave entertainment to local Maori with a vigorous and bitter theological debate. Ordained a deacon in 1844, Colenso became the most influential Pakeha figure in early Hawke's Bay. Under instructions from the Bishop of New Zealand, George Selwyn, he travelled in the region over the summer of 1843–44, and surveyed the length of the east coast from the Wairarapa north to the top of Hawke's Bay before returning to the Bay of Islands by way of a second crossing of the Urewera. He went on to establish the first Hawke's Bay mission and, between 1845 and 1852, explored routes across the Ruahines to the head of the Rangitikei River and became the first European to make the crossing from Hawke's Bay to Lake Taupo.

Small numbers of British settlers began to arrive in both Poverty Bay and Hawke's Bay in the early 1850s, when the outpost of Napier was established at Bluff Hill. Development of the entire region was slow, as the great forests were painstakingly felled and burned to make way for sheep farming. Communications were never easy and the east coast's connection with the rest of New Zealand was by sea for many years. Although a coach service made the arduous journey between Napier and Wellington from 1868, the rail connection was not finished until the 1890s, and the line from Napier to Gisborne was not completed until the 1930s.

The East Cape–Poverty Bay–Urewera region has always been remote from the major urban centres of the North Island, not only in physical fact but also in the imagination – a land of contorted hills, winding roads and distant bays encompassing a withdrawal or separateness from the changes that have governed the development of the rest of the country. Separateness goes back to 1840 and the Treaty of Waitangi, which many chiefs of the region refused to sign. The first New Zealand governor to visit the east coast, in 1860, was received with little ceremony. The Land Wars that flared up in Taranaki that year arrived in the east in concert with the fanatical Hauhau religious sect, leading to particularly brutal fighting in 1865–66. When government forces prevailed, land was confiscated and 330 Maori prisoners were exiled to the Chatham Islands.

Among them was Te Kooti Arikirangi, unjustly accused of being a spy. At the Chathams, Te Kooti claimed to have visions that led to his leadership of Ringatu, a new Old Testament-style

ABOVE: *Napier from Bluff Hill in the early 1870s, showing the town situated between the sea and Ahuriri Lagoon. The 1931 earthquake drained the lagoon, providing land for new suburbs.*

RIGHT: *Rua Kenana established a messianic movement in the Urewera in the early part of the twentieth century, establishing laws and codes of practice for Maori in opposition to Pakeha government. He stands (third from left) above his circular courthouse and meeting house at Maungapohatu in 1908.*

faith. A charismatic and violent leader, he engineered an astounding escape from the Chathams and returned with his followers to Poverty Bay. Between 1868 and 1872 he proved the scourge of Te Urewera and Poverty Bay, conducting brutal guerrilla warfare against Pakeha and his tribal enemies. His forces were finally defeated and he sought sanctuary in the King Country with only a handful of followers. Eventually he made formal peace with the government, was pardoned in 1883 but continued to lead a turbulent life until his death 10 years later.

Gisborne as a town was not surveyed and named until after the threats from Te Kooti had disappeared in the 1870s. While the communities and farms of Hawke's Bay grew steadily and unhindered after the mid-1860s, resistance to Pakeha settlement and the rule of government continued in parts of the Poverty Bay–East Cape region and especially in the Urewera, where the scorched-earth policy of government forces, in retribution for Tuhoe support of Te Kooti, had left deep suspicion, resentment and hardship. The condition of the Tuhoe yielded the messianic movement of Rua Kenana, who, at the isolated Urewera settlement of Maungapohatu in 1907, established a 'New Jerusalem' with its own laws and codes of practice. Conflict with the authorities was inevitable and Rua was imprisoned in 1917. He rebuilt Maungapohatu in 1927, but his vision of finding a way of community for his people in the new Pakeha-dominated world faded with his death a decade later.

Sheep farming on great stations became the dominant productive activity across all the plains and hills of the east coast lands. Its towns, later cities, grew as service, processing and shipping centres for the wool and sheep meat grown on these hinterlands. Hawke's Bay in particular became known as a rich pastoral province, supporting a gentry whose only peers owned the great sheep stations of North and South Canterbury. Its towns – Napier, Hastings and Havelock North

LEFT: *Herbert Guthrie-Smith's homestead on Tutira station shortly before his death in 1940. Guthrie-Smith's book* Tutira *was a classic work of natural history, recording the massive changes to the northern Hawke's Bay landscape brought about by the advent of sheep farming.*

– were named for heroes of the Indian Raj, reflecting the nineteenth-century settlers' strong sense of Empire.

The clearance of forests in southern Hawke's Bay, however, presented a more formidable challenge, one that made Scandinavian immigrants weep when they confronted the task in the 1870s. Much of the great 'Seventy Mile Bush' of virgin podocarp forest was destroyed in terrible fires as the land was wrenched and scorched into farms. The labours and the ancestry of the Scandinavian settlers of this region are commemorated in the towns of Dannevirke and Norsewood. Sheep farming was not always a prosperous occupation for gentlemen, and neither easy on the farmer nor the land; and from northern Hawke's Bay came a chronicle of change that stands as a monument to the colonial farming experience.

Herbert Guthrie-Smith took up Tutira station in 1882 and, apart from developing the station to a holding that covered 60,000 acres by the end of the 1890s, began 40 years of detailed observations of his environment that culminated in his great 1921 publication *Tutira: The Story of a New Zealand Sheep Station*. Guthrie-Smith continued his observations and completed a revised edition before his death in 1940. In this most detailed of natural histories, he recorded the 'ruin of a Fauna and Flora unique in the world – a sad, mad, bad, incomprehensible business'.

> *The difference between Tutira of '82 and Tutira of 1939 is the difference between youth and age: the face of the one smooth, that of the other wrinkled and lined. In the early days of the station its surface was unmarked by paths; now it is seamed with [sheep] tracks . . . the station was an untrodden wild . . . in the language of Scripture, void; its surface is now a network of lines; it is reticulated, like the rind of a cantaloupe melon.*

ABOVE: *The massive earthquake that shook Hawke's Bay on 3 February 1931 reduced much of Napier to rubble; 256 people were killed in the worst natural disaster to strike New Zealand since European settlement.*

From the summit of Panekiri Bluff, above Lake Waikaremoana, one may look north to the many inlets and bays of the lake, set in unblemished arms of forested spurs and hills, green-black trees rolling as far as the eye can see. To the south, however, the scene is almost of disaster, where the hills have been laid bare by felling and burning. Everywhere the land is ravaged by the white scars of erosion, unstable land crumbling without the support of root and branch. This famous double-sided view is the most vivid example of the devastation wrought on hill country all across New Zealand by the indiscriminate clearance of forest in the 'mad, bad' pursuit of profit that Guthrie-Smith so vividly recorded for posterity.

In 1931 Hawke's Bay experienced a different kind of devastation when it was the locus for the biggest natural disaster to occur in New Zealand since European settlement. At mid-morning on 3 February a huge earthquake tore apart Napier and Hastings, killing 256 people. The shock and subsequent fires effectively destroyed both towns, causing damage of about £7 million. The tremors of the country's greatest catastrophe were recorded on the other side of the world and scarred the countryside from Wairoa south to the Wairarapa. Yet there was considerable compensation. Before the event Napier had clustered about Bluff Hill, a coastal margin and the edge of the Ahuriri Lagoon to the north. The earthquake drained and lifted the lagoon bed, returning 3340 hectares of land from the sea and providing space for new suburbs such as Marewa ('raised from the sea') and Pirimai ('joining up'). Napier still has the look of a new city and, because it

was reconstructed during the 1930s, its buildings give it the distinction of being the 'Art Deco Capital' of New Zealand.

Sheep farming for wool and meat dominated the economy of the East Coast–Hawke's Bay region until after the Second World War. But the foundations for the area's currently rich viticultural and horticultural industries had already been laid. Despite early climatic difficulties, the *Phylloxera* aphid scourge in the early years of the twentieth century, the propaganda effects of the temperance campaigns in the 1920s, and then the economic blows of the 1930s Great Depression, a winemaking industry was established and slowly thrived. The Mount St Mary's Mission vineyard is the oldest in the country and has been producing wine from Greenmeadows since 1897. Vidal's vineyard was established at Hastings in 1905 and, later, grapes were planted at Te Mata Estate, the oldest commercial winery in New Zealand. Hawke's Bay and Poverty Bay now produce about a third of New Zealand wines, contributing significantly to one of the country's fastest-growing domestic and international markets.

The largest and most diverse food-processing factories in the Southern Hemisphere started with a Hastings backyard cannery built by James Wattie in 1934. Today, many thousands of hectares of Hawke's Bay farmlands produce vegetables for canning and freezing that are exported to more than 40 countries. The Heretaunga Plains area is often described as the 'Fruit Bowl' of New Zealand for its annual production of more than 100,000 tonnes of pip and stone fruits. In

ABOVE: *New Zealand's first vineyards were planted in Hawke's Bay more than a century ago. Today the eastern North Island region accounts for about a third of the country's wine production.*

handling the industries based on this vast benison of horticultural production, there has long been a rivalry between Hawke's Bay's twin cities, with Napier as the exporting and business centre, and Hastings home for the major processing industries and their concomitant agricultural and pastoral shows and blossom festival. Napier remained the more populous centre until the 1960s, boosted by its secondary role as a popular seaside resort, but since then the development of the horticultural industry has seen Hastings match its sister. Gradually the cities are physically merging so that this conurbation, including Havelock North, has reached a population of 130,000 – the fifth-largest urban area in the country.

Hawke's Bay projects an image of sun-soaked orchards, vineyards and market gardens – a kind of New Zealand Tuscany, but a Tuscany with the additional attribute of a great sweep of golden-sanded coast that has pulled holidaymakers from all over the North Island for many years. The brilliant coves and sands of East Coast–Poverty Bay draw travellers – campers, surfers and fishers – in search of coasts even more remote. Much of this country still has the feel of Witi Ihimaera's semi-mythical Waituhi:

> *. . . dust and more dust, the constant characteristic of Maori country . . . a road with houses on either side and, in their back yards, the best maize, kumara, pumpkin and watermelon crops this side of Heaven.*

In the mountains behind both bays lies the dark and glittering heart of this land, Waikaremoana. Brooding or stormy among the old and heavy hills of Te Urewera National Park, it holds the essence of what this land once was when the 'Children of the Mist' first entered its forests, echoing to the bell tones and flashing feathers of the kokako and long-extinct huia.

ABOVE: *A giant northern rata (Metrosideros robusta), a choking hardwood liana that transforms itself into a tree. Te Urewera National Park.*

LEFT: *Waikaremoana, 'Sea of Rippling Waters', is the dark and glittering heart of the Urewera, land of Tuhoe, 'Children of the Mist'.*

WELLINGTON & WAIRARAPA
WIND & CURRENT

WIND & CURRENT

THE POLYNESIAN demi-god hero Maui fished up all the islands of the Pacific but his biggest catch by far was the North Island of New Zealand. His canoe – the South Island – was already overloaded with fish but, ignoring his brothers' protests, Maui smeared his fish-hook with his own blood for bait and cast it over the side, chanting a karakia that gave him the power to haul up the world. The waka nearly capsized as Maui pulled in his enormous final catch, Te Ika a Maui, (the Fish of Maui), the entire North Island. He took it home for the tohunga to lift its tapu before the giant fish was eaten, but his brothers were greedy and began to cut it up at once. The fish twisted and lashed about with the anger of the gods at such sacrilege, creating the contorted landscape of an island that would otherwise have been as gently undulating as the scaly form of the living fish.

The mouth of Te Ika a Maui remained forever open at the island's southern limit, inhaling and exhaling deep breaths in its last dying gasps, creating the constant winds and currents that continue to swirl about in the narrow waters lying between the fish's head and the side of Maui's canoe.

Polynesian myth accords nicely with the palaeogeographical record. The North Island did rise and fall, twist and contort through the eras of geological time. Over the past 50 million years only the region of the Coromandel Peninsula has remained always above the sea. The twisting of the fish was caused by the constant folding and buckling of sedimentary rocks along the junction of the Pacific and Indo–Australian Plates, as well as widespread volcanic activity.

At the height of the last major ice cycle, sea levels retreated so far that the North Island's South Taranaki Bight was dry and merged with the South Island's Tasman and Golden Bays, forming a

PRECEDING PAGES: *The wild shores of Cook Strait on Wellington's south coast.*

LEFT: *Before earthquake uplift in 1855 and harbour reclamation, flat land was at a premium in the Wellington settlement. Ten years after the future capital's founding, its buildings clustered on Te Aro Flat or along the water's edge.* (S. Brees)

ABOVE: *The Brooklyn Hill wind turbine demonstrates how much power is free on a Wellington wind: gusts up to 250 kph have been recorded in the vicinity. Farms of turbines have been established in nearby Wairarapa.*

RIGHT: *Charles Heaphy's view of*
Wellington in 1841 projected
the image of an ideal planned
settlement for New Zealand
Company propaganda. It shows
one of the town's calmer days, the
hills are not noticeably steep and
the harbour is a haven for all the
navies of the world.

vast plain with rivers draining into the South Pacific. As sea levels rose again, the ocean flooded over the plain and through the southern hills to create a 25-kilometre-wide funnel for fast-flowing tides and westerly winds. It was named Raukawa by Maori – Many Reefs – for the numerous rocks, islets and underwater reefs that litter the strait Captain Cook eventually named for himself.

Movements along the series of fault lines that run the length of New Zealand from the Bay of Plenty to Fiordland caused the sinking of valleys adjacent to the faults, filling them with sea water, and one of these became the gaping mouth of Maui's fish, today's Wellington Harbour. The Polynesian navigator Kupe was reputed to be the first to visit the harbour, naming its two islands Matiu and Makaro after young female relatives. The first Maori to settle here came with Tara, the son of Whatonga of the *Kurahaupo* waka: the tribe become known as Ngai Tara and the harbour Whanganui-a-Tara – the Great Harbour of Tara.

While Maori settlement about the harbour, and the nearby west and east coasts of the lower North Island, was continuous from the fourteenth century, the rugged landscape and stormy coasts did not support the substantial populations found in more favoured regions to the north. Seafood was plentiful, but few areas were suitable for kumara growing, except along the warmer coast opposite Kapiti Island. The harbour and the Kapiti coast were also the launching sites for invasions of the South Island as hapu after hapu moved into the region in successive movements of population from north to south.

Abel Tasman in 1642 did not discover the gap between the islands and sailed on north. While Cook proved the shape of the North Island by sailing through the strait in 1769–70, he missed the

great harbour, and paid just a brief visit on his second voyage three years later. The entrance was narrow, protected by Raukawa, and the winds were unpredictable and often violent. The harbour only became a regular port of call after Captain Herd visited in 1825 and reported, 'The navies of all the nations of the world could lie at anchor here.' He named it Port Nicholson after Sydney's harbourmaster, and this was abbreviated to 'Port Nick', or 'Poneke' to the Maori.

By the time of Herd's visit there had been recent disruptive changes to local Maori populations. Musket invasions by the Waikato had driven Taranaki iwi, such as Te Ati Awa and Ngati Mutunga, south to the margins of Cook Strait, and later Ngati Toa, after conflict with the Waikato, migrated from Kawhia, led by their great fighting chief Te Rauparaha. In the 1830s unrest and tensions between the different tribal groups precipitated destructive raids into the northern South Island marshalled by this 'Maori Napoleon'. In 1835 Ngati Mutunga decided to move on from the strait region and seized a visiting Australian brig, the *Lord Rodney*, forcing its skipper to take them to the Chatham Islands. Here they took the indigenous non-violent Moriori people into slavery, which led to their extinction a century later.

On to this unsettled and volatile tribal scene came the good ship *Tory* in September 1839. It carried with it instruments of change the like of which the Raukawa region had never seen before, despite all the wars and migrations of the past. The New Zealand Company, at the behest of its ideological mentor, Edward Gibbon Wakefield, had sent out an expedition under his brother Colonel William Wakefield to 'possess yourselves of the soil' for new British colonies, before the British government took control of New Zealand as a Crown colony.

Obtaining land cheap from Maori to sell dear to British settlers and investors would raise the

ABOVE: *When British settlers
arrived to take up their sections at
the new Wellington settlement, they
found Maori still in occupation of
key sites, such as Pipitea Pa.
Disputes over land, leading to
armed conflict, were not settled
for seven years. (W. Smith)*

capital to fund planned settlements with a balanced cross-section of society. The money would
also fund the immigration of labourers, and Maori would benefit by their being allocated a tenth
of the subdivided land and sharing in the growth of its capital value. The trouble was, this was
not the Maori way with land. Also, this first settlement had been planned in detail in London –
down to the subdivision of town and country sections – without any idea of where it would be
and the character of the local landscape. The first ships loaded with emigrants – 900 men, women
and children – set out from England before any news had been received from William Wakefield
about his success or otherwise, in order to meet with him at a prearranged rendezvous in Cook
Strait on 16 January 1840. Such folly, such courage, such faith. This is how the 'organised' British
settlement of New Zealand began.

With muskets, blankets and other trade goods, William Wakefield 'bought' millions of acres
of land from Raukawa region Maori that encompassed much of the lower North Island and

LEFT: *There was insufficient agricultural land in the vicinity of Wellington to cater for the economic needs of the new colony. Enterprising settlers crossed the eastern ranges to the Wairarapa basin and found sufficient land to establish sheep stations. (W. Smith)*

upper South Island. His deals were assisted by tribal rivalries and the desire of Maori to see Europeans settle among them with their new industrial-age goods and weapons. They had no conception of the scale of British migration that was planned. Wakefield confirmed Captain Herd's opinion of Port Nicholson as the best harbour of the region and sited the first Company settlement there.

The colony was soon named Wellington, after England's military hero, and most of the other features in the vicinity were renamed to commemorate the supporters or directors of the New Zealand Company in an early example of sponsors' naming rights. Matiu Island was renamed for the Company chairman, Joseph Somes; Makaro for its secretary John Ward. Wellington had a great harbour, a bracing climate and wonderful scenery, but very little flat land for the farms needed to make the colony viable, except in the adjacent Hutt Valley. However, the settlers confidently expected that centrally located Wellington would be chosen as the country's capital,

ABOVE: *Lack of communications through the steep hill country between Wellington and the Wairarapa limited development of the region until the rail connection was completed with the use of Fell steam engines on the 1-in-15 Rimutaka Incline. (J. Gully)*

RIGHT : *The CBD of Wellington city today, looking towards the boat harbour, Oriental Bay and Mount Victoria - and the Rimutaka Ranges, which lie beyond the eastern side of the harbour entrance. The high-rise buildings beyond the first row, and Te Papa National Museum at right, are all built on reclaimed land.*

bringing the economic benefits of hosting government and its administrative services. But Governor Hobson's choice of Auckland for the capital, inadequate investment and a weak economic base, disputes and then outright war with Maori over land, all contributed to a staggering start for Wellington during its first decade.

The settlement inexorably developed according, not to the Wakefield grand plan, but to local needs and conditions. As early as 1842 scientist Ernst Dieffenbach, no friend of the Company, could write:

> *Nearly three years have elapsed since our first visit; and a spot scarcely known before that time, and rarely if ever visited by Europeans, has become the seat of a large settlement, with nearly 5000 inhabitants . . . a town with warehouses, wharfs, club-houses, horticultural and scientific societies, racecourses – in short, with all the mechanism of a civilized and commercial community; at this very place, where I then enjoyed in all its fulness the wild aspect of nature . . . there is now the restless European, spreading around all the advantages and disadvantages of civilization and trade.*

After the Maori had been subdued militarily, the Wellington settlement found more stability and prosperity with the move of pastoralists into the adjoining Wairarapa basin beyond the Rimutaka Ranges to the east. The Hutt Valley was cleared and farms spread up the Kapiti coast. Shortage of flat land and communications difficulties with the hinterland were ameliorated by a whopping earth movement in 1855 along the great fault line that runs down the western shore of the harbour. Coastal land in the area rose by as much as one and a half metres, and both the harbour bed and a submerged shelf were raised up. A platform for a new Hutt Road and railway line had been gratuitously provided; easier access around the coast to the Wairarapa; more land for the city and shallower waters for reclamation, which was to reach massive proportions. The city's main thoroughfare of Lambton Quay marks the original shoreline of 1840: the greater part of the current central business district, all the city's wharves and container terminal, railway station and yards, motorway and sports stadium lie on land uplifted by earthquake or claimed from the sea since 1855.

By the 1860s most of the land in the Wellington region and in the Wairarapa/southern Hawke's Bay had come into Pakeha hands and the city began to prosper commercially as the port and business centre for a pastoral economy. But the biggest stimulus to Wellington's growth came when its citizens' clamour to have the capital shifted from Auckland finally brought a result. By 1864 the total Maori population – mostly in the northern part of the country – had diminished to about 53,000, while the Pakeha population had increased speedily to more than 170,000. Two-thirds of these were in the South Island, consequent on a booming pastoral economy and the gold rushes in Otago and Westland. The case for a capital central to the spread of population and economic activity became inarguable and was reinforced by the South Island's threat of secession – a call heard from time to time in later years whenever 'mainlanders' thought the capital (and

ABOVE: *The site of Wellington's, and then the nation's, governance has always been sited on the Thorndon rise above the harbour's original foreshore. The Beehive executive wing (left) stands on the site of William Wakefield's and then the first governors' houses. The marble Parliament Building was completed in 1922, without a planned left wing and dome.*

Auckland) took them and their superior resources far too much for granted.

Wellington became the capital in 1865 and grew rapidly as the governmental administrative centre, attracting numerous commercial and financial enterprises. Its power grew with the abolition of provincial governments in 1876 and the improvement of communications with the lower North Island. Steep, winding roads were engineered through Wellington's encircling hills, providing links from the harbour and the Hutt Valley to the Kapiti coast and thence to the Manawatu and, more improbably, over the Rimutakas into the Wairarapa. The first railway from Wellington made its way up the Hutt Valley in 1874, and then into the Wairarapa in 1878 by virtue of the famed 1-in-15 Rimutaka Incline, where specially constructed Fell steam engines designed to grip a centre rail took goods and passengers over the 500-metre divide to Featherston. The incline carried rail traffic until 1955 when a nine-kilometre rail tunnel was completed.

Until the 1870s the Wairarapa was home to a score of sheep stations that waxed fat on the open fern and grass lands that the pioneering sheep farmers had discovered in its southern basins. The advance of the railway brought resources into central and northern Wairarapa and settlers

LEFT: *Green pastures and exotic shelterbelts have replaced the dense native forests that once covered this countryside near Martinborough in the Wairarapa.*

began clearing the vast virgin podocarp forests for its building timber and farmlands. As the railway pushed on, new towns sprang up beside it – Featherston, Carterton, Masterton and, in the 1880s, north to Eketahuna and Pahiatua.

The character and atmosphere of this northern Wairarapa country in the late nineteenth century – and of all North Island areas being relentlessly cleared of their ancient native forests for farms – was vividly captured in Arthur Adams's 1904 novel *Tussock Land*:

> *It was land yet in the dismal half-cleared state that the train ran through . . . and the eternal succession of bleached or blackened corpses of trees, the sodden trunks lying where they had fallen, the sparse green that was but beginning to assert its healing kindness, the ugly little whares of the struggling settlers, the bleakness of the railway-track through this avenue of newly-slain trees, the muddy road among which the carters laboured behind their teams of five . . . the unkempt children that stood on the barbed-wire fences of the sections and waved at and cheered at the passing of the train – all this gradually sent a feeling of depression over him. He was coming to a country where life did not go so easily . . . here the struggle was undisguised and bitterly strenuous. There was no trifling with the imperturbable strength of Nature; there was no repose, no sloth in the wrestle with that unwounded foe. Work was the word this country said – Work!*

And work the pioneering farmers did, up and down the length of the North Island, turning black bush into the sheep and dairy lands on which came to depend the country's prosperity as the British Empire's finest farm.

ABOVE: *The railway link between the Manawatu and southern Hawke's Bay follows the precipitous geological quirk of the Manawatu Gorge. It took several years to lay 10 kilometres of track.*

As the railway reached out to these lands in the Wairarapa, southern Hawke's Bay and up the west coast to Manawatu, Wanganui and Taranaki, the capital city grew and grew as an international export/import terminus and the focus of the nation's railway, shipping and, much later, air services. Wellington remains the country's busiest port, partly by virtue of the Cook Strait ferry trade.

Linking Wairarapa on the east with Manawatu on the west is the quirky geological phenomenon of the Manawatu Gorge. The Manawatu River rises in southern Hawke's Bay but, instead of flowing east into the Pacific Ocean, it swings hard right through the dividing Ruahine Range and then flows over the Manawatu plains into the Tasman. Geological explanations for this strange gorge are not conclusive, but Maori myth is. In the Puketoi hills where the river rises, the gods invested a sacred totara with the capacities of an eel. Wriggling forcefully and blindly down the riverbed, the great totara would not be deflected by the hills and simply battered its way through to the sea! Like Cook Strait further south, the Manawatu Gorge funnels every wind going and the river's turbulent currents remain a challenge to canoeists. The difficult and dangerous task of constructing a road through the 10-kilometre-long gorge took the best part of two years in the early 1870s; at the most difficult points, workmen were suspended from clifftops with ropes to hack out the road platform. The railway line, with tunnels, and linkage with the Wairarapa and Hawke's Bay lines, was not completed for another 20 years.

The most important Pakeha settlement in the Manawatu in the early days was Foxton, founded in 1855. Close to the mouth of the river and the long beach routes to the north, it became the largest township between Wellington and Wanganui, the focus of a thriving flax industry. Like the Wairarapa, the Manawatu plains were covered in dense bush and were attractive to prospective runholders and farmers. But their purchase and development did not take place until after the founding of Palmerston North, in an inland bush clearing in 1866. Again the pattern of fell and burn, with the aid of an advancing railway, progressively turned the forest into farms.

The rivalry between Foxton and Palmerston North to become the hub of the Manawatu was settled in 1886, when the Main Trunk line, which had inched its way up the coast from Wellington, finally reached Palmerston North, bypassing Foxton on its way to Auckland. Foxton had the compensation in the twentieth century of being squarely astride State Highway 1. Road traffic north then bypassed 'Palmy'. But Palmerston North developed independently as an agricultural service, manufacturing and research centre, and grew to vie with Tauranga as the sixth-largest city in New Zealand. Massey College, founded in 1928 just outside town, was only the second tertiary institution in the country to be devoted solely to agricultural sciences. It has since become a full-scale university with an extra campus north of Auckland. The Palmerston North locality is also home to seed testing, grassland, artificial breeding and dairy research institutes.

Despite harbour reclamation and planting suburbs over steep hills and into improbable gullies, the site of Wellington could not contain the growing population of a capital city. The Hutt Valley was first cleared of forest and turned into farms and market gardens to feed Wellington. But Petone and Lower Hutt became towns in their own right and, in the twentieth century, the site for extensive industrial development and state housing schemes. Here was room for a racecourse, an army camp and the dormitory suburbs for Wellington's army of bureaucrats. Similar suburban development, with a heavy emphasis on state housing schemes for urban Maori, took place after the Second World War in Porirua, Tawa and Titahi Bay, over the hills to the north-west.

By the end of the twentieth century, with the population of this Greater Wellington reaching 350,000, the Hutt Valley was almost entirely built over. Improved highways and suburban train services extended commuter suburbs as far up the Kapiti coast as Waikanae, 60 kilometres distant, and to the fashionable Wairarapa lifestyle towns of Featherston, Greytown and Martinborough, up to 90 kilometres away. The Wairarapa had become a wine-growing district, hosting memorable food and wine festivals. Wellingtonians seeking a weekend away from it all

ABOVE: *Wellingtonians visit a fair at Martinborough. The small towns of the Wairarapa have become both long-distance commuter suburbs to the capital and the focus for wine-related festivals and fairs.*

Above: Castlepoint lagoon and lighthouse, a favourite Wairarapa destination for Wellington weekenders. Horse-race meetings are held annually along its wide beaches.

travel out to the coast at Castlepoint, Riversdale and Lake Wairarapa to enjoy the fishing.

Residents of the Kapiti coast enjoy ocean beaches and views, most notably of brooding Kapiti Island, redolent of myth and ancient wars. Once Te Rauparaha's stronghold – he tussled with William Wakefield aboard the *Tory* in the roadstead between the island and the Waikanae shore – Kapiti is now a renowned bird sanctuary, refuge for species that were victims of the massive changes made to forests on the mainland.

The Kapiti coast has a milder climate than Wellington's, which soon became known as the 'Windy City'. Missionary Richard Taylor, as early as 1855, encapsulated the character of both Wellington's climate and its politics:

> *Party spirit has always run high in this settlement, but it is generally acknowledged that this is chiefly owing to the high winds, which render the minds of the settlers so irritable, that, were it not for the politics, which act as the safety valve of the place, there is no saying what would be the result. It has been remarked that those living in the most exposed positions suffer most, and become the bitterest politicians, whilst others who have selected more sheltered localities, are the least acted upon by these barometrical changes.*

Joking apart, hurricane-force winds are regularly recorded at climate stations on Wellington hilltops and the city has the highest mean wind-speed flow of any urban centre in New Zealand. Storms combined with the fast and violent currents that swirl about the coast from Cape Terawhiti to Turakirae Head can create major hazards for shipping. Cook Strait ferry sailings from Wellington to the South Island are regularly delayed or cancelled because of weather or sea conditions, and one of the worst maritime disasters in New Zealand's history occurred in 1968 when the ferry *Wahine* became the victim of ferocious winds and giant seas as she entered the harbour and hit reefs near the entrance: 51 died. Strong winds and a shortish runway at Wellington airport also often make a flying visit to the capital the most exciting travel experience

ABOVE: *Brooding Kapiti Island, off Wellington's west coast, was once the stronghold for the great Maori warrior chief Te Rauparaha. Now it is a wildlife sanctuary, where kiwi and native parrots thrive, free from introduced predators and grazing animals.*

ABOVE: *The Cook Strait suburb of Island Bay shows how a shortage of flat land means that most of Wellington's sea margins and hill crests have been colonised for housing the capital's growing population.*

in New Zealand. Yet Wellington in many ways simply reflects the character of most of New Zealand – hilly with spectacular seascapes and an unpredictable, invigorating climate. There is no sky as blue, no atmosphere as clear and almost surgically clean as Wellington's on a still morning following a southerly storm.

Wellington's notorious winds, its cramped location and its image of boring politics and grey bureaucracy led to a longstanding joke (probably originating in rival Auckland) where the first prize for the winner of a competition was a night in Wellington, the second prize was two nights in Wellington, and the third prize was three nights in Wellington. But this joke has been consigned to the dustbin since a new and burgeoning café culture has combined with the vigorous growth of New Zealand artistic identity during the closing decades of the last century to make Wellington the cultural as well as political capital of the country.

Home to the New Zealand Symphony, Ballet, Arts Council, National Library and numerous

other cultural institutions, the capital supports a political, bureaucratic and diplomatic élite that provides a discerning audience for an increasing level of artistic performance and exhibition. Wellington's theatre is the most vibrant and innovative in the country, and its biennial international festival of the arts has become the equal of any in the Southern Hemisphere.

In 1998 New Zealand's new national museum – Te Papa – was opened on the Wellington waterfront. It created immediate controversy: over its architecture, which was likened to a warehouse or aircraft hangar; and for its curatorial philosophy of presenting New Zealand's history and culture in the manner of a trade expo. Yet its millions of visitors since opening testify to Te Papa's popularity with the New Zealand public, who perhaps see in its energetic commingling of the sacred and the profane, the Maori and the Pakeha, the ancient, the modern and the post-modern, a vivid metaphor for the state of a nation discovering and celebrating its own identity in an increasingly globalised world community.

ABOVE: *Wellington's Civic Square, the cultural centre of the city, embracing the old town hall and concert chamber (centre), Michael Fowler concert hall (left) and the city library and art gallery.*

NELSON & MARLBOROUGH
SUN TWINS

SUN TWINS

THOUGH STRIKINGLY DIFFERENT in landscapes, and separated by steep hill country, the provinces of Nelson and Marlborough have long been combined in the New Zealand imagination. They are joined by a common location that makes them separate from the rest of the country, even from the rest of the South Island, and by a common pattern of discovery, migration and settlement. Encompassing the head of the South Island, most of the Nelson–Marlborough region straddles the same latitudes as the southern North Island, and the two provinces are linked by 740 kilometres of the most beautiful and accessible coastline in New Zealand. These warm coasts persistently face north, and the provincial capitals of Nelson and Blenheim compete only to see which one records the nation's highest annual sunshine record!

Geologically the region is demarcated by the great Alpine Fault and its associated fractures that mark the line of the Awatere and Wairau Valleys. South-east of these the rocks are dominantly greywacke and schist sedimentaries. Yet, north-west of the silts of the Tasman Bay basin, the entire top corner of the South Island is dominated by a granitic complex of rocks, closest in character to Fiordland, and clear evidence of sideways movement along the Alpine Fault over millions of years.

Much of Nelson–Marlborough is mountainous. The only flat or gentle lands suitable for agriculture lie about the main river valleys and coastal margins, though the dry hill country of Marlborough has proved amenable to sheep farming. Inland, the lakes of Rotoiti and Rotoroa mark the basins of long-gone glaciers at the northern extremity of the Southern Alps, which here clear 2300 metres in height. The Alps disperse about the line of the Alpine Fault into the

PRECEDING PAGES: *Sheep country beneath the Seaward Kaikoura Range, Marlborough.*

LEFT: *Many of the bays in Abel Tasman National Park provide safe haven for sea kayakers exploring the golden coves and granite reefs and headlands of this warm and sheltered coast.*

ABOVE: *Approaches to Waiau Pass, Nelson Lakes National Park. The back country of Nelson–Marlborough affords innumerable opportunities for hunters, trampers, fishers and mountaineers.*

FAR LEFT: *The splendour of Golden Bay's remote beaches: Wharariki Beach and Archway Islands near Farewell Spit.*

LEFT: *The view from Mount Stokes (1203 metres) over Queen Charlotte Sound to Arapawa Island, Cook Strait and the Wellington coast of the North Island. The importance of this Sound as a haven for Captain Cook's ships during his three round-the-world voyages is marked by the naming of Endeavour Inlet.*

highlands of Marlborough, lifting the Inland Kaikoura Range to 2885 metres at the summit of Tapuaenuku, the highest mountain north of the Mount Cook district. The Richmond Range, lying between Marlborough and Nelson, and the summits of the remote ranges of north-west Nelson reach 1800 metres. Dry and bare in the east, wet and forested in the west, the mountainous back country of Nelson and Marlborough is a Mecca for the hunter, tramper, kayaker, skier and mountaineer.

In contrast to the high and rugged interior, the coastal margins from Farewell Spit in the north to Blenheim in the south are a beachcomber's or sea tramp's paradise – a succession of golden beaches, sheltered tidal estuaries, secluded bays and, above all, the sunken sea-flooded river valleys of the Marlborough Sounds, whose 380 kilometres of shoreline encompass waterways and anchorages to delight even the most jaded mariner's heart.

The warm and sheltered coastal enclaves of Golden Bay, Tasman Bay and the Marlborough Sounds – and the access they gave to rich fishing grounds – were coveted destinations for all those Maori tribal groups forced south by war or new immigrant invasion from the favoured Iwitini lands in the upper part of the North Island. While most of the South Island was under the control of Ngai Tahu by the eighteenth century, the north-west long claimed a separate tribal identity. Here the land had been first settled by Ngai Tara, first inhabitants of Wellington Harbour, and they had been followed in the eighteenth century by Ngati Tumatakokiri, who then held sway over the Nelson (Whakatu)–Golden Bay (Wainui)–West Whanganui region for the following 200 years.

ABOVE: *The Ngati Tumatakokiri*
warriors who attacked Abel
Tasman's men in Golden Bay
in December 1642. Tasman's
expedition never set foot on
'Nieuw Zeeland' soil.

Ngati Tumatakokiri were the people who, populating Taupo Pa at the south-east corner of Golden Bay, watched the strange spectacle of two giant single canoes with sails like small clouds approaching the shore on 18 December 1642. Suspecting a war party, Ngati Tumatakokiri put out two double-canoe loads of warriors to ascertain the strangers' strength and intentions. Encountering men of unknown costume and colour in 'canoes' larger than any they had seen before, the warriors blew conch shells to signal their alertness and readiness for attack. The ships of the Dutch East India Company's exploring expedition had unwittingly anchored in a tapu fishing ground. The waka returned to shore to the answering blare of tinny trumpets.

Next day the expedition commander, Abel Janszoon Tasman, offered gifts to men in the first Tumatakokiri canoes to stand off his ships *Zeehaen* and *Heemskerck*. But they did not respond, and later a force of 80 warriors in several canoes ran down the *Heemskerck*'s cockboat, killing four of Tasman's men. The Dutch explorer sailed out of what he termed 'Moordenaers Baij' without obtaining fresh food and water, and the savage experience inhibited him from attempting to land again in the country his employers named 'Nieuw Zeeland'.

The reputation of the killers of 'Murderers' Bay' caused James Cook to avoid a close acquaintance with the Tumatakokiri coast. On January 1770 he discovered instead the perfect anchorage for the long-distance voyager in the haven of Ship Cove, within the entrance of the sea sound he named Queen Charlotte after the consort of England's reigning King George III. The bush-sheltered setting of Ship Cove provided fresh water and firewood, a shelving beach to careen his ships, and a pleasing environment for the rest and recreation of his men. Cook visited Ship Cove on all three of his voyages – undeterred by the massacre of men from the *Adventure* at Grass Cove in 1774. Here he claimed the South Island for England, released the first pigs and goats, planted the first European vegetables and, from a hill on Arapawa Island, first saw that there was a strait between New Zealand's two islands.

After 1800 Ngati Tumatakokiri control of the north-western coasts was broken. Ngai Tahu attacking from the south and Ngati Apa from the north reduced the tribe to a fragment by the time French navigator Dumont d'Urville visited Tasman Bay in 1827 and dealt with them during his first scientific survey of the area. In negotiating the passage between the mainland and the large island that came to be named after him, d'Urville almost lost his ship amid the ripping currents and reefs, leading to its soubriquet, French Pass. Just a few months after d'Urville's visit, a new invasion of the region began, by Taranaki iwi in concert with Ngati Toa chief Te Rauparaha, who was raiding into the Marlborough Sounds and down the east coast of the South Island. Ngati Tumatakokiri were slaughtered, scattered and enslaved, their tribal mana and whakapapa absorbed forever by the invaders.

At about this same time Europeans began regularly visiting the South Island's Cook Strait coast. The first to stay were whalers, most notably John Guard, who from 1828 established shore whaling stations at the entrance to Tory Channel and in Port Underwood. By the time

missionary Samuel Ironside (the second in the South Island) arrived here, concurrently with the New Zealand Company ship *Tory* in 1839, Pakeha and local Maori had intermarried in settled whaling and trading communities at the edge of the sounds. William Wakefield dealt for control of all Nelson–Marlborough land for the Company, but while Te Rauparaha was to concede he had sold Whakatu (Nelson) to 'Wideawake', he held fast to the wide and empty Wairau Valley, which ran down from the Southern Alps and into the strait at Cloudy Bay.

William Wakefield's brother Arthur, a naval hero, led the second New Zealand Company expedition into Tasman Bay in 1841 and named the new settlement after his own hero, Horatio Nelson. There was a splendid sun-soaked site for the new town but a lack of the alluvial plains or downlands necessary for the success of an agricultural settlement. Even the acquisition of land in 'Murderers' Bay' across the Takaka Hill did not meet requirements. The bay was now renamed 'Coal Bay' for the first recoverable coal deposit to be worked in New Zealand, but this was superseded by 'Golden Bay' after the discovery of gold in 1857. 'Golden' now has come to apply to the

ABOVE: *Whaling continued until the 1960s from the Te Awaiti shore station, first established in 1828 at the entrance to Tory Channel. Here, in 1918, a humpback whale has been hauled up for flensing.*

ABOVE: *The site for Nelson was*
chosen where a long boulder bank
gave shelter for shipping in the
south-east corner of Tasman Bay.
The first settlers found the immedi-
ate foreshore already cleared from
earlier Maori occupation, but there
was little flat land or easy downs
country essential for the success of
an agricultural settlement.
(C. Heaphy)

bay's endless fine beaches where the sand's granite-derived components truly glitter.

Nelson surveyors found a pass from the inland lake of Rotoiti to the Wairau Valley and declared its unoccupied plains and surrounding hills as ideal for pastoral settlement, solving the new settlement's problems. William Wakefield said he had bought the Wairau; Te Rauparaha said he had not sold it. Arthur Wakefield believed his brother. Claim, counterclaim and dispute reached a tragic climax in June 1843 when a group of armed settlers confronted a Ngati Toa taua (war party) at Tuamarina in the lower Wairau. Twenty-two Nelsonians were killed, including Arthur Wakefield and other settlement leaders, and four Maori died. While Governor FitzRoy found no fault with the Maori and no Pakeha retribution was demanded, the 'Wairau Affray' was the first incident of violent conflict over land that was to disfigure New Zealand's race relations over the next 30 years.

Progress of the Nelson settlement was set back for years by the Wairau incident. Farming development of the valley itself did not begin until it was formally purchased under Governor Grey in 1847. Land communication with Nelson remained long and difficult, and Marlborough,

named for yet another English military hero, became a separate province in 1859. This precipitated comic-opera local politics over which town – Picton in Queen Charlotte Sound or Blenheim on the Wairau plain – should be the provincial capital. The same massive earthquake in 1855 that lifted up more land for Wellington had depressed land in the lower Wairau by as much as two metres, deepening the Opawa River and improving shipping access to Blenheim. The 'capital' shifted back and forth between the two towns, depending on which political faction was in power, until the province went almost bankrupt and Picton, Pelorus and Kaikoura moved to separate in 1868. Marlborough staggered along until the abolition of provincial government in 1876, when the government buildings in Blenheim appropriately went up in smoke.

Although there was a gold rush to Golden Bay in 1857 and the Wakamarina at the head of Pelorus Sound in 1864, the workings were short-lived. There were some modest industrial developments in both Nelson and Blenheim in later years, but these and the overall growth and prosperity of both provinces came to depend on pastoral farming, horticulture, timber milling and, since the Second World War in particular, tourism. Consequently the region has never supported large resident populations: Nelson City passed 50,000 only in the mid-1990s, while Blenheim's population has reached only half that number. Population of the entire region from Farewell Spit to Kaikoura amounts to just 125,000.

German settlers came to join British in the Nelson settlement soon after the Wairau incident, contributing early wine-growing skills in an area where complex soils and a variety of balmy microclimates led to a rich horticultural farming belt. Nelson became the apple orchard of New Zealand; the Motueka region became the country's tobacco field and grew the best hops to flavour New Zealand beers. The orchard and garden atmosphere of Nelson with its copious sunshine attracted smallholders, alternative lifestylers and 'greenies' and from among these came many artists and craftspeople. Nelson was one of the centres from which the cottage pottery

ABOVE: *Captain Arthur Wakefield (1799–1843), one of Edward Gibbon Wakefield's younger brothers, was the leader of the Nelson settlement and his organisational and leadership skills overcame many of the deficiencies of the New Zealand Company operation. His death, along with that of other Nelson luminaries, in the clash at the Wairau in June 1843 set back the settlement's progress for a decade.*

LEFT: *A view of the Wairau River, lagoon and coast near Blenheim in 1869, during the fractious days of provincial government. (J. Richmond)*

ABOVE: *The sunny and sheltered Nelson region has long been a land of orchards and horticultural groves, producing pip fruit, hops, berries and kiwifruit. In an earlier era, Motueka was New Zealand's chief tobacco-producing area.*

RIGHT: *A vast Marlborough wine estate near Blenheim. Although wines have been produced here only within the last 30 years, the region now yields almost half of New Zealand's total production, principally chardonnay and sauvignon blanc.*

industry expanded quickly across New Zealand in the late 1960s and 1970s, and the quality of the region's weaving and jewellery-making soon attracted national attention. More recently, Nelson's annual Wearable Arts Awards has drawn international praise for its craft and innovation.

Nelson's climate has long attracted the retired and family holidaymakers from the northern half of the South Island and southern North Island. Seaside 'bach' settlements such as Kaiteriteri and Torrent Bay have become synonymous with the image of the long lazy days of summer. Beyond the steep Takaka Hill, Golden Bay is even more identified with sun and sand, as a remote and idyllic place to get away from it all. At the extreme tip of the region, walking along the great 25-kilometre-long Farewell Spit as the sun goes down, one has the sensation of walking along the very edge of the world. Nearby Whanganui Inlet has the primeval feel of original New Zealand – the way it was before humans arrived and irrevocably altered the landscape. For some, Golden Bay has become the ideal place to escape the industrialised world. More than half the current population are immigrants from polluted and overcrowded Europe.

The Takaka Hill region between Tasman and Golden Bays is famous for its granites and limestones. Its coastline is a necklace of granite caves, pillars, arches and reefs. The highland quarry of Kairuru yielded the marble to build Wellington's Parliament and Nelson's cathedral. And beyond the quarry, among the rocky outcrops of the Pikikiruna Range, are a warren of potholes to challenge the world's bravest underground explorers.

The coves, inlets, estuaries and hills of this region were declared a national park in 1942, 300 years to the day after Tasman provoked the ire of Ngati Tumatakokiri. Abel Tasman National Park (22,500 hectares) is one of three to grace the Nelson area. The vast Kahurangi National Park (452,000 hectares) encompasses the entire north-west corner of the South Island and is traversed by one of New Zealand's most famous walking tracks, the Heaphy, which takes travellers from Golden Bay to the nikau palm coast of northern Buller. Nelson Lakes National Park (102,000 ha) is equally accessible from Marlborough, and embraces Lakes Rotoiti and Rotoroa, both popular with boaties and anglers.

Although Marlborough province boasts no national park, more people visit the Marlborough Sounds than any other part of the top of the South Island. This is partly because Picton, though losing the contest to be provincial capital, has long been the region's premier port, the South Island terminus for Cook Strait ferries making the three-hour-plus voyage to and from Wellington via Tory Channel. Since 1962 the roll-on, roll-off ferry links have provided the most important freight, and only vehicular and rail wagon, connection between the two islands. At Fighting Bay, not far south of the entrance to Tory Channel, is the terminus for another kind of link. Here the Cook Strait cable enters the sea, providing an umbilical of power for northern cities and industries from South Island hydro-electric stations.

Picton has thrived around the ferry transport nexus and as a boating and yachting harbour for those who set out to explore, holiday and fish as far as Cook's Ship Cove at the mouth of

ABOVE: *Groves of nikau palms* (Rhopalostylis sapida*) grace the coastal section of the famous Heaphy Track, which crosses Kahurangi National Park from Golden Bay to Karamea on the West Coast.*

ABOVE: *Picton, in Queen Charlotte* Queen Charlotte Sound or to Anakiwa at its head, the base for New Zealand's only Outward
Sound, is the South Island terminus Bound School. Pelorus Sound's port is Havelock, astride the road between Blenheim and Nelson.
for Cook Strait vehicular ferries, More difficult of access, Pelorus is also vastly more complex than Queen Charlotte, a maze of side
which provide the watery link for sounds, reaches, inlets, arms and coves that reward years of exploring holidays. Many of its shel-
State Highway 1, stretching from tered reaches have become the ideal sites for mussel farms.
Cape Reinga in the north to Bluff   The Marlborough Sounds are wet and windy, vintage Cook Strait country. But by far the great-
in the south. est part of the province, south of the Wairau River and blocked between the Spenser Mountains and
the east coast, stands high and dry, in prevailing westerly rain shadow and receiving little rain even
from southerlies. Much of this country is arid mountain land over 600 metres in height and is
suitable only for high-country farms grazing a handful of Merino sheep or hardy cattle to the
hectare, such as the great 182,000-hectare Molesworth station at the head of the Awatere Valley. But
in the district around Blenheim, the dry climate and high sunshine hours, coupled with irrigation,

have seen since 1980 the establishment of the largest wine-growing industry in New Zealand, especially in the production of premium white wines such as sauvignon blanc and chardonnay.

The tens of thousands of travellers toing and froing from the Picton ferries each year all motor along State Highway 1 through the new vineyards and, further south, they pass another Marlborough industry founded on the arid climate. Lake Grassmere within the lee of Cape Campbell – the South Island's most easterly point – is the site of a solar salt works encompassing 688 hectares of seawater ponds that, with the aid of locally high evaporation rates, yield all of New Zealand's industrial and table salt requirements.

ABOVE: *Dry-cattle lands in the Wairau Valley, inland from Blenheim.*

RIGHT: *Crayfish and whales populate deep waters fingered by the Kaikoura Peninsula. The best marine highway in the country traverses this mountainous coast.*

The highway wriggles through the parched hills south of Blenheim before reaching the sea again at the Waima River. It then leads the motorist along the most spectacular marine drive in the country. To the east, the swells of the South Pacific Ocean break heavily against precipitous bluffs and rocky headlands and reefs favoured by colonies of fur seals. To the west, rugged hills rise steadily to the snow-capped heights of the Seaward Kaikoura Range, where Marlborough comes to its conclusion at the Kaikoura Peninsula. Town and fishing port stand only 20 kilometres distant from the 2600-metre peak of Manukau and offer the most dramatic sea–mountain setting of any settlement in New Zealand.

Kaikoura is named for its plentiful supply of koura – crayfish. Its abundant seafood resources and the rare anchorage it has provided along the long coast invest the spindrifting haze along the coast with the smell of history, both Maori and Pakeha. Old myths and old wars, and the old destructive industries that slaughtered this coast's seals and whales, have given way today to a reverence for the marine life that enriches Kaikoura's waters. Visitors now watch the dolphins and whales that enjoy the unusually deep but sheltered waters off the peninsula. The emblem of this coast is no longer the raised patu or lance, but the lifting of a great humpback tail above the black waters, figured against the high snows of Manukau.

WEST COAST
WILD & WET

WILD & WET

MENTION 'THE WEST COAST', or even 'the Coast', to anyone in New Zealand and it will be taken to refer to only one place – that long and narrow strip of country running the length of the South Island between the Main Divide of the Southern Alps and the Tasman Sea. Some of the (few) inhabitants of this isolated region tend to be a little more picky, however, and will tell you that there are really two parts to the West Coast: Buller, which takes in that country between Karamea in the north and Greymouth in the south; and Westland, which runs south of the Taramakau River all the way down to Awarua (Big) Bay. The Buller has significant alluvial river valleys, lower mountains and a slightly milder climate. But all of it is wet, mostly wild, and Coasters have a reputation for making up for their isolation with a particularly robust kind of hospitality. Not for nothing is it claimed that those little mats for soaking up spilled beer are named for this West Coast tradition.

The West Coast has never been a human-friendly zone. The region comprises mountains, more mountains, hills and a coast that stretches for more than 500 kilometres without a natural harbour, open to ocean swells that have been driven 2000 kilometres across the Tasman Sea by prevailing westerlies. These westerlies dump copious amounts of rain. The town of Hokitika (where residents claim it only rains during the night) averages more than 2800 millimetres a year. But nearby alpine regions receive two to three times as much, and produce the fastest and most dangerous rivers in New Zealand.

Before humans came, the West Coast was all river and swamp at the valley floor and coastal margin, then wet forest to the subalpine grasslands at about 1200 metres, which quickly turned

PRECEDING PAGES: *Pancake Rocks blowhole at Punakaiki, Buller coast.*

LEFT: *Silver beech (*Nothofagus menziesii*) forest beside the Oparara River, near Karamea.*

ABOVE: *The wild west coast north of Greymouth.*

to rock, scree and shattered summits reaching higher than 3000 metres. In the south, the mountains were covered with fields of permanent ice and snow, remnants of the last ice age, with glaciers like the Fox and Franz Josef tumbling through wicked gorges right into the sea. The further south, the closer the mountains creep to the coast, until Aoraki/Mount Cook – just east of the Main Divide at 3753 metres – stands only 30 kilometres away. Coasters say its summit casts a shadow on the sea on a clear morning's sunrise. As Denis Glover's poem 'Arawata Bill' put it:

> When God made this place
> He made mountains and fissures
> Hostile, vicious, and turned
> Away His face.

Yet there is some flat land in the middle of all this, especially adjacent to the main river valleys such as the Taramakau, Grey and Buller in the north. But the persistent rains tend to leech and bog the soils, and if farmers turn their back for a moment, it seems, on pastures laboriously cleared and drained, they revert quickly to scrub, heading for the dank beech and podocarp forests whence they came. New Zealand's tallest trees, kahikatea (white pine), thrive in such country, their great grey trunks rising from roots buttressed against the swamps at their feet. But though it was 'wicked country . . . there was gold in it for all that'. The human history of the Coast has long revolved around the exploitation of its precious mineral resources.

The region was inhospitable to neolithic Polynesian settlers accustomed to warmer climes and more fertile soils. But one part of the West Coast held the greatest prize for a stone age culture. In about the fifteenth century, early Maori explorers, reputedly Ngati Wairangi, discovered greenstone in the Arahura River, nephrite jade that for its hardness, beauty and cutting edge had no peer in Aotearoa. Ngati Wairangi traded the precious stone north through the only river route that penetrated the Alps, the Buller, to iwi in the Cook Strait region and the North Island. The jade was called pounamu and the South Island became known as Te Wai Pounamu (Greenstone Waters). By the seventeenth century, when Ngai Tahu had taken control of the eastern regions of the island, Ngati Wairangi found accessible summer passes across the Southern Alps to trade with them. Eventually Ngai Tahu slaughtered Ngati Wairangi or took them as slaves to carry blocks of stone on the long and dreadful marches across the mountains. The West Coast branch of the Ngai Tahu who came to inhabit the 'greenstone pa' at Arahura and nearby Taramakau became known as Poutini Ngai Tahu, after the legendary green taniwha, or sea monster, whose dying transformation in the bed of the Arahura created the greenstone lode.

The first European to sight New Zealand, Abel Tasman, made his landfall off the West Coast just south of present-day Westport and found 'a large land, uplifted high', but with no prospect of a safe anchorage or welcoming settlement. In 1770 Captain Cook described it as 'an inhospitable shore', and in 1826 one of Dumont d'Urville's officers thought it 'one long solitude with a forbidding sky and impenetrable forest'. By the time Europeans began to arrive in numbers in the

South Island from 1840, a half-dozen or more greenstone routeways across the Southern Alps from the east coast had been proved by Ngai Tahu. But the tribe's numbers had now dwindled to about only a thousand, and no more than a few dozen occupied the Poutini pa. Their knowledge was not accessible to English surveyors, and the West Coast remained a vast and dark mystery to the new settlers.

After the Wairau incident in 1843, Nelson settlers looked south to find the pastoral lands needed to sustain the new colony, and early in 1846 young surveyors Charles Heaphy and Thomas Brunner were sent off to explore the West Coast. Their guide was Kehu, one of the few Ngati Tumatakokiri who had survived the Taranaki iwi invasion of the north-west 15 years before. Heaphy and Brunner made a remarkable five-month return journey from Golden Bay, all the way down the rough and precipitous West Coast from Farewell Spit to the Arahura River greenstone pa. They were the first Pakeha to travel on the Coast and the first to see the mountain known as Aoraki to Ngai Tahu and soon to be named Cook by the hydrographer J. L. Stokes.

While this journey seemed to prove that no useful pastoral land lay within easy reach of Nelson, Brunner was determined to return and prove the full course of the Buller River, explore the entire West Coast as far as Milford Sound, and then prove a pass over the Southern Alps to the east coast. He set off with Kehu again at the end of 1846 but was given up for dead when he had not returned a year later. Brunner nearly did die, of a stroke. He finally staggered back to the Nelson settlement in June 1848, suffering from the destruction of all his clothes, footwear and equipment in a journey that had taken him through the horrors of the Buller Gorge and the river-riven coast as far south as Paringa. Injury and threat of desertion by his Maori companions had prevented his going further south or crossing the Alps, but he had explored the Grey Valley on his return and discovered coal in its lower reaches. Brunner had completed the longest journey of exploration in the European history of New Zealand.

Following Brunner's report that the West Coast had not been 'worth incurring the expense of exploring', there was no Pakeha interest in the region for a decade. In 1860 the government finally got around to purchasing the Coast from local Maori for £300. Posting a reward for a payable gold find in the new settlement of Canterbury, which then included the West Coast, had also provoked the search for passes across the Alps. The government survey depot at Mawhera (Greymouth) was about to close when the strike finally came in July 1864. The rush was on. Within a year a coach road across Arthur's Pass had been constructed and the new canvas and façade town of Hokitika supported a digger population of 6000, which it has not equalled since. The Coast's 1860s population of 26,000 was not much less than it is today.

The main rush for alluvial gold was finished after three years, but finds continued on the beaches of the long coast, from Westport to Bruce Bay, and among quartz reefs in Buller's Inangahua. Here the town of Reefton was founded – the first in the Southern Hemisphere to be lit by electricity, from a mine hydro station in 1888. The Reefton district yielded claims with the

ABOVE: *Thomas Brunner and Charles Heaphy, with their Ngati Tumatakokiri guide Kehu, crossing the Buller River near present-day Murchison, February 1846. Brunner and Heaphy's journeys into the Buller and West Coast region began as an attempt to find pastoral farming lands for the Nelson settlement. (W. Fox)*

colourful titles of Keep-It-Dark, Just In Time and Fiery Cross when gold recovery had become the business of dredging and mining companies. The spirit of those golden times is preserved in Shantytown, near Greymouth, a re-created nineteenth-century rush town. And there has been a resurgence of gold recovery in recent times as modern machinery and techniques allow good profits from finer dredging of old claims.

Although timber began to be cleared for farms from the flatlands about the Buller rivermouth and the middle Grey Valley, farming has contributed only modestly to the West Coast's boom-and-bust economy. As gold extraction went into decline, the next rough quarrying of the earth for its resources began – the extraction of coal to feed the homes and industries and steam engines of New Zealand's cities. Quality bituminous coal was found in the lower Grey Valley and in the ranges north of Greymouth and Westport. Production began in the 1870s, and reached its peak between 1880 and 1920, when Buller produced 60 per cent of all New Zealand's coal. Westport became the biggest coal port in the country. One of the outstanding engineering feats of the coal age was the cableway of the Denniston Incline. Using the counterbalancing dynamics of full and empty trucks down a gradient as steep as 1-in-1.34, 30 million tonnes of coal were shipped via the cableway over 88 years from 1880, down 600 metres from the edge of the coastal plateau to the main Westport railway line beneath.

The close-knit coalmining communities proved to be the breeding ground for radical and trade union politics. 'King Dick' Seddon, premier of New Zealand from 1893 to 1906, started his career as mayor of Kumara and became the miners' representative in Parliament. He personally

ABOVE: *Over about 90 years from 1880, 30 million tons of coal were shipped down the renowned 1-in -1.34 Denniston Incline to the coastal railway north of Westport. All goods traffic made its way up and down in the counterbalanced hoppers – and sometimes people, too.*

directed the rescue operations during New Zealand's worst-ever mining disaster, when 67 men and boys were killed in the Brunner mine explosions of 1896. The Labour Party had its roots in the strong coalmining union movement that developed on the Coast in the years that followed. West Coast coal production declined after the First World War as hydro power and petroleum fuels came into their own, and as the coal needs of Auckland were met by the closer mines of the Waikato. But mining continues today, mainly of high-quality anthracite for export.

Gold, coal and, later, timber extraction led to a rail link between the West Coast and Christchurch/Lyttelton that was completed with the opening of the Otira Tunnel in 1923. Roads improved over Arthur's Pass, down the Buller Gorge and via the Lewis Pass. But the major

highway improvements, including the opening of the Haast Pass route, have come as a conse-quence of the West Coast's real and lasting wealth – its magnificent scenery and natural environ-ments, which each year attract hundreds of thousands of tourists from all over the world.

Julius von Haast, Canterbury's provincial geologist in the 1860s, was the first to draw atten-tion to the West Coast's natural wonders. In 1863 he made the first crossing of the Haast Pass from Otago to South Westland, and in 1865 was the first to examine and describe the Fox and Franz Josef Glaciers, which at that time cascaded into bushlands to within 300 metres of sea level. They became one of New Zealand's premier tourist attractions for those willing to tackle the rough country south of Hokitika, with its numerous big river crossings, on foot and horseback. A fully bridged motor road reached the glaciers by the early 1950s, but it was the opening of the Haast Pass road in 1965 that started the motorised tourist boom. The townships of Fox and Franz Josef have also long been bases for high climbing and tramping, especially over the Main Divide Copland Pass track leading to Aoraki/Mount Cook.

The third major extractive industry – the cutting of native timber for building and furniture – has been progressively phased out by successive governments who have perceived the special value of the West Coast's remaining extensive forests. Less than 20 per cent of the native forest extant in New Zealand when British settlement began in 1840 still survives, and most of this can

ABOVE: *The Morning Star gold claim in operation behind the main street of South Westland's Ross in 1870. In 1866, two years after the rush started, it was reported that there were as many holes in the ground around Ross as 'a nutmeg grater'. The biggest gold nugget ever to be found in New Zealand was unearthed here: the 100-ounce 'Honourable Roddy' ended up as Buckingham Palace tableware.*

ABOVE: *Franz Josef Glacier, Westland National Park. Huge nevées high in the Southern Alps collect the snow that compresses under its own weight to form this slow-moving cascade of ice. The glacier tumbles down to about 300 metres above sea level, close to the forest.*

be found in the western half of the South Island (including Fiordland). Much of the New Zealand forest biota is unique, and the scale of the unaltered West Coast landscapes, especially south of Hokitika, make them an increasingly valuable resource for science and for tourism, of both the passive and adventure type, in a wider world whose natural forests and wild landscapes are rapidly being destroyed.

The value of this priceless resource has been marked by the progressive gazetting of national parks and reserves, so that the West Coast region has more of its territory under protection than any other part of the country. International recognition of the region's special natural qualities came in 1990 when the entire south-western part of the South Island, incorporating Aoraki/Mount Cook, Westland, Mount Aspiring and Fiordland National Parks, was declared the Te Wahipounamu World Heritage Area, comprising a tenth of New Zealand's entire land area.

The Buller region also can now boast two national parks – the southern part of the Kahurangi, bordering the warm Karamea coast, and Paparoa embracing the ranges between the Grey Valley and the sea. Paparoa is remarkable for the caves, chasms, potholes and coastal

ABOVE: *Paparoa National Park in Buller is a fascinating riddle of water-carved limestone caverns, tunnels and potholes.*

LEFT: *The Buller River thunders into its upper gorge. Explorer Thomas Brunner took eight weeks to make its first descent, a journey now covered by car in less than an hour.*

blowholes of its variegated limestone country. Additionally, most of the rugged hill country of the Buller and Grey River watersheds, and its vast beech forests, are also under Crown reserve. New Zealand's third national park, Arthur's Pass, encompasses parts of the Main Divide region of the Taramakau watershed, its connecting road riding a spectacular viaduct above the Otira Gorge.

The jewel of the Coast's parks is Westland/Tai Poutini, running down from the highest peaks of the Southern Alps, where it merges with Aoraki/Mount Cook park on the east, all the way to the coast – from Mount Tasman (3496 metres) to Gillespies Beach. It incorporates the great Franz Josef and Fox Glaciers. The northern road approach, through avenues of native rimu and kahikatea trees and beside bush-dark lakes, eases the traveller into the gigantic natural vistas of the World Heritage zone. From lookouts at Okarito Lagoon, on the coast just north of Franz Josef, one can gaze over unblemished forests to the icy Alps and along the wild coasts to the north and south and imagine with ease a world before humans. Here one can feel only awe and humility before the power of nature.

The waters of Okarito Lagoon, and its great forests and surf-beaten coast, epitomise all that is grand about natural Westland, and it seems entirely appropriate that near here is the only New Zealand breeding ground of the white heron – the kotuku, elegant, rare and sacred to the Maori. The rich feeding grounds of the lagoon, including the delicacy of tide-running whitebait, are vital to the kotuku colony and to many other sea and shore birds.

The small settlement at Okarito is a reminder of the tenuous human history of this coast. When explorer Thomas Brunner rested here in 1847, it was the southernmost settlement used by

ABOVE: *In September, whitebait run the gauntlet of fishers' nets through the entrance to Okarito Lagoon. Rich in bird and fish life, the lagoon was the southernmost summer settlement for West Coast Maori. Beyond lay only wilderness, most of which remains today within the protection of national parks.*

Poutini Ngai Tahu, valued then, as now, for its whitebait fishing and birding resources. Beyond was a wild land, fit only for travellers. But in the 1860s Okarito became a gold-rush town for diggers exploiting the sands of nearby beaches. It once had a population of several thousand served by three banks, a courthouse and 31 pubs.

It was from Okarito that South Westland's greatest historical figure, 'Mr Explorer' Charlie Douglas, set off on his legendary journeys of exploration into all the unknown mountain valleys between Okarito and Jackson Bay. The folkloric wisdom of his writings has become a watchword on the Coast, dry sayings that encapsulate both the character of the place and its stoic inhabitants. He survived 40 years of exploring this impossible country and when asked how he had escaped drowning in one of its terrible rivers, he commented, 'Not being able to swim has saved my life

many a time,' knowing that it was usually the brave, the foolhardy (and the drunk) who drowned. He told travellers impatient with endless days of rain, 'It's no use tapping the glass, man. The barometer doesn't affect the weather much on the Coast.'

Charlie Douglas was also one of New Zealand's first conservationists. In 1891 he lamented the rapid loss of native birds: 'The Digger with his Dogs, Cats, rats, Ferrets and Guns have nearly exterminated [them] in the lower reaches of the southern rivers.' And he hid information he had collected on mineral resources to prevent further reckless exploitation of the land. In the wonderful natural world of South Westland, we are still able to contemplate the truth in Charlie Douglas's words of more than a century ago: 'Fools think that Knowledge can only be got from books & men.'

CANTERBURY

THE EDGE OF A CONTINENT

THE EDGE OF A CONTINENT

EARLY POLYNESIAN VOYAGERS would have recognised islands of ancestral memory in the contorted green hills and blinding sands of North Island bays and hinterlands. But those who first coasted along the eastern margins of the South Island, their sailing waka scudding before the raging gusts of a warm nor'west gale, would have found something new in their oceanic experience. Beneath skies heavy with grey whales of cloud, and mountains like ocean breakers higher than any in imagination, lay a land too high and wide and too extreme in climate to accord with the idea of an island. They had come to something beyond easy understanding. It was less an island than the edge of a continent.

The South Island is no larger than Greece, but the scale of its landscapes show that it is indeed the distant outrider of that old continent, Gondwana. The great Alpine Fault and the upthrust of the Southern Alps – Ka Tiritiri o te Moana, Gift of the Sea – dominate the 800-kilometre long island. The Alps form the Main Divide between the narrow and precipitous strip of the wild and wet West Coast and the dry foothills, downlands and plains of the east. The island is made up of the mountains' buckle and dross, and they also create the weather, contour the sky, dictate life and the passage of humans.

The largest portion of this mountain-shadowed landscape, encompassing the most considerable plains in New Zealand and its most extensive montane prairies, has become known as Canterbury. Bounded on the west by the highest peaks of the Southern Alps, on the east by endlessly curving Pacific coasts, its northern and southern margins are the long braided courses of the Waiau and Waitaki, two great Canterbury rivers that trace their source to alpine snow and ice.

PRECEDING PAGES: *Lake Tekapo in late winter, Mackenzie Country, South Canterbury.*

LEFT: *Sunrise on Aoraki, Hooker Valley, Mount Cook National Park.*

ABOVE: *Distinctive nor'wester wave clouds above the hot dry hills of inland Canterbury near Arthur's Pass.*

RIGHT: *Great braided rivers, such as the Waimakariri, carry down silt and gravel from the mountains to form the Canterbury Plains, one of the biggest shingle fans in the world.*

As the working of the fault continues to uplift the Southern Alps, glaciers grind them down and their rivers carry away the silt and gravel, spilling from foothill gorges to form one of the biggest shingle fans in the world. Banks Peninsula, jutting from the east coast like a battered and scarred greenstone mere, was once an island, lifted from the sea in a volcanic upheaval 30 million years ago when the Alps lay distant across a 60-kilometre-wide strait. But the extending fan of shingle steadily filled in the gap; the junction was complete by the time the first Polynesians put ashore.

At first the dry forests of the plains were exploited by hunters pursuing flocks of grazing moa. Fires and dogs were used to herd them into the culs-de-sacs of coastal estuaries, where they were slaughtered on such a scale that within a couple of centuries this entire race of birds was extinct. After the age of moa hunting, Waitaha people were supplanted by Ngati Mamoe invading from the north and the 900-metre-high Banks Peninsula became the most favoured locus of settlement. Much of the South Island was too cold for Polynesian settlement, but the peninsula was warm and well watered from coastal rains, clothed in dense forest and margined by lagoons and swamps, all as rich in birds as the coastal margins were in seals, dolphins and fish. Kumara and karaka could grow in its warm bays; its headlands were suited to fortified pa.

By the late eighteenth century, Canterbury – and most of the South Island – had come under the control of hapu associated with another invading tribe, Ngai Tahu, who had built their major pa at Kaiapoi (just north of today's Christchurch). A few hundred Poutini Ngai Tahu lived close to greenstone (pounamu) sources across the Southern Alps and a web of Maori routeways from Kaiapoi led to passes across the Alps, attesting to its trading value. By Captain Cook's arrival, every iwi in the country had obtained the chiefly taonga of pounamu ornaments.

On his map of New Zealand, Cook showed Banks Peninsula as an island – rather late after the event – and his mistake was not discovered until 1809, when the first British sealing ship sailed by. Over the following 30 years European sealers, whalers and traders began to visit with increasing frequency, and the first shore whaling stations were established in the mid-1830s. The arrival of Europeans coincided with the self-destruction of the Ngai Tahu iwi when, in 1824, a careless breach of protocol against paramount chief Te Maiharanui set up a chain of internecine cannibalistic killing that became known as Kai Huanga, the 'Eat Relation' feud.

By 1830, torn apart and demoralised, Ngai Tahu now became prey to Ngati Toa warrior chief Te Rauparaha, who led raiding parties south across Cook Strait from his stronghold on Kapiti Island. Hundreds were killed and pa devastated as the war raged back and forth over the next decade. In 1820 Canterbury had a Ngai Tahu population of about 3000 people; in 1840 it was just 600, a total that was to be further depleted by new European diseases such as measles and tuberculosis. Ngai Tahu were also now easy prey for European land speculators and dictatorial government agents. By 1848 almost the entire South Island had passed to the Crown and European landowners for a few thousand pounds. Just 2575 hectares had been reserved for the 647 Ngai

ABOVE: *Akaroa, Banks Peninsula, became the first European colony in the South Island when a small group of French settlers arrived in 1840. Today it is a holiday resort with Gallic flair.*

Tahu still living in the southern half of the island, and they had been turned off many of their traditional settlement sites. The iniquities and indignities inflicted on Ngai Tahu at this time were not recompensed until the settlement of the Ngai Tahu claim under the provisions of the Waitangi Tribunal in 1998.

The first permanent European settlement in Canterbury was a French colony established at Akaroa in 1840. Although the French government hoped that this might be the basis for wider French settlement of the South Island, and perhaps a sovereign French colony, the enterprise was altogether too half-hearted to succeed. When Charles Lavaud, 'Commissaire de Roi', arrived in the Bay of Islands in July to herald French settlers, he discovered that the Treaty of Waitangi had been signed and the whole country declared a British Crown colony. Governor Hobson immediately sent officials to Akaroa to hold court and raise the Union Jack to dispel any alternative plans that Lavaud might have still had in mind. The French colony never grew, largely because its site gave little room for agricultural development and, for many years, access was possible only by sea. For

all the warmth and beauty of its natural location, Akaroa was destined to remain a charming Gallic oasis within a Britannic New Zealand.

The empty plains were a more logical site for a new colony. And in provoking the formation of the Canterbury Association – a colonising venture sponsored by Church of England luminaries – Edward Gibbon Wakefield found a last chance to implement his theories of colonisation, based on planned settlements with a balanced mix of squire, merchant, artisan and labourer. The scheme attracted disgruntled young English gentry with hopes of privileged usefulness; the shabby but genteel lower middle class with ideas of making a fortune; and the labouring poor with the prospect of work, dignity and eventually some land of their own.

The first Canterbury Association settlers – the 'Pilgrims' – arrived in Lyttelton Harbour on the 'First Four Ships' just before Christmas 1850. Along with wheel and plough, sickle and churn, they brought English names to extinguish the Maori, along with their title to the land. Christchurch was to be the chief town, and Avon its winding river. From the crest of the Port Hills

ABOVE: *The port of Lyttelton about seven years after the founding of the Canterbury settlement at the end of 1850. The communications difficulties between the port and the future city of Christchurch on the Canterbury Plains were solved by the opening of one of the world's longest railway tunnels in 1868.*
(J. Bunney)

Right: *Horsley Downs, North Canterbury: a sheep-station scene from the late 1860s. At this time, about half of New Zealand's sheep population was being grazed on Canterbury's plains and downlands. Sheep runs were unfenced and flocks were controlled by boundary-riding shepherds working from remote huts.*
(H. Lance)

the new arrivals looked over the vast Canterbury Plains, dissected by the glittering braids of the great Waimakariri River, and for one insane moment renamed it Cholmondeley ('Chumley'). They saw, according to poet Arnold Wall,

> *. . . league upon league, hill, plain and spur,*
> *Of grass of the colour of weasel's fur,*
> *Of leafless bushes and sedges harsh*
> *And ragged forest and reedy marsh . . .*

where their unimaginatively planned city would be.

It took longer than expected to establish the ideal settlement of Christchurch market town, with an Anglican Church establishment and schools, served by a prosperous agricultural hinterland. There were too many speculators, too few labourers and not much from which to earn an income. Cathedral, manor and a chequerboard of wheatfields became no more than a dream when the nearest big market was Australia and the greatest export was labour bound for the Victorian goldfields. Little labour, less market meant a change of plan. Orderly migration, surveyed city and the right people with the right outlook were nought without cash. The Victorian gentlemen who led the colony saw what must be done. Their duty to the settlement's wellbeing, their obligations to endow the Church, the pressing need to save themselves from economic death, conjured up salvation on four hooves. There was deliverance in the sheep's dull eye, and profit from its back as wool exports boomed.

By June 1853 Canterbury had a hundred sheep runs over an area of a million acres. By the end of 1854 all the plains and front faces of the foothills were taken, and by 1856 most of the high

country, Merinos dribbling into the long hard valleys of the Alps. In 1851 there were just 15,000 sheep, but only 10 years later Canterbury led the nation with 877,000 of New Zealand's total flock of 2.7 million.

Around that time Samuel Butler, author of *Erewhon*, was exploring the alpine valleys, looking for new sheep country, and in the Harper tributary of the Rakaia River gave the landscape typical pioneer treatment. He thought that the 'bush, though very beautiful to look at, is composed of nothing but the poorest black birch'. So he set it on fire '. . . and made a smoke which was noticed between fifty and sixty miles off. I have seen no grander sight than the fire upon a country which has never before been burnt . . . The sun loses all brightness, and looks as though seen through smoked glass.' Butler admitted, 'Our object was commercial not scientific; our motive was pounds, shillings and pence.'

The fires of the sheep farmers swept over the entire plains and foothills of the Southern Alps, incinerating most of the native plant cover, destroying entire bird species such as the native quail, completing the alteration of the vegetative cover begun by Maori centuries before. Sheep

ABOVE: *The view north from the top of the Bridle Path between the port of Lyttelton and Christchurch on the Canterbury Plains, 1861. Pegasus Bay curves away to the north-east. (J. Swayne)*

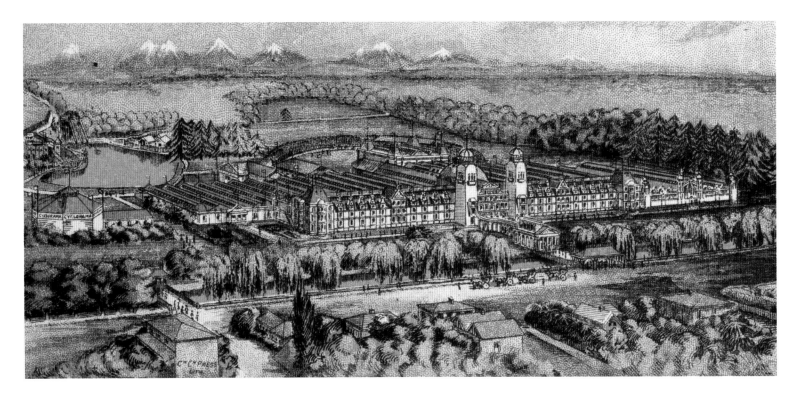

continued the change as they grazed over the landscape like maggots on a decaying carcass, and exotic mammals such as rabbits were let loose to make a thorough job. Scores of unnamed animal and plant species were lost and many others placed under threat. In concert with the burning of the runs, axe, saw and fire played like a maniacal trio as the forests of Banks Peninsula and North Canterbury were felled to build the growing city of Christchurch. In 1851 the peninsula was two-thirds covered in bush; by 1900 hardly a native tree was to be found across the lowland reaches of the province.

Sheep and timber were not the only roads to a quick return. As the Australian market grew, the plains became a vast field for bonanza wheat cropping. The land was broken by man, horse and plough until the hot and dry nor'wester took the soil away in fine clouds of dust sweeping past the city to the sea. The best part of a century passed before the robber ethics of the colonial frontier gave way to a more conservative and sustainable farming economy. By then the province had become established as the agricultural and pastoral heartland of the country. The central place of farming to the Canterbury economy was reflected in the establishment of New Zealand's first agricultural college (later a university) at Lincoln in 1880. Canterbury's easy geography, its farming resources, and lack of competition with Maori, meant that the settler colony had the least troubled course of development of any part of New Zealand.

Christchurch grew steadily as the market, retail and industrial centre for the province, reflecting country wealth and pride. Timaru was its minor counterpart for the subprovince of South Canterbury. Farming prosperity saw the building of Christchurch Cathedral begun in the 1870s; its spire was up by 1881 and the last stages completed in 1904. Museum, Christ's College,

provincial chambers and university rose in matching English Gothic and, outside the four avenues of the city proper, nondescript suburbs were built to accommodate an increasing population of shopkeepers and industrial workers. Oliver Duff, first editor of the *New Zealand Listener*, once wrote about Christchurch that

> *. . . there has always been conflict between squatters and shopkeepers; between a minority, predominantly Church of England, who had land and some education, and a majority, largely Methodist, who followed trade and said "baa" to the wool kings . . .*

While Christchurch and Canterbury still project watery echoes of the English class system, the city also has a proud reputation for radicalism, labour politics and unionism springing from the other side of the railway tracks in the industrial south of the city.

Rail, steam and agricultural mechanisation gave Christchurch companies an early reputation

ABOVE: *Christchurch in the 1920s, looking down the main north–south thoroughfare of Colombo Street towards Cathedral Square. For more than 100 years after its founding, Christchurch fulfilled its original Wakefieldian role as the market town – a retail, service and educational centre – for its rich agricultural hinterland.*

for engineering prowess. In 1861, just 10 years after the founding of the colony and when the combined population of Christchurch and its port of Lyttelton was merely 5000, the first sod was turned for a great tunnel through the hill from the city to the harbour. Two years later the first steam locomotive in New Zealand clattered from Christchurch to the tunnel workings, and in 1868 one of the longest railway tunnels in the world – at two and a half kilometres – was opened for business. A two-kilometre-long rail bridge across the Rakaia River was completed in 1873 as railways snaked out from Christchurch to bring people and produce from all corners of the province to market.

Through crop field and sheep paddock, through shelter belts of foreign pine, eucalypt and macrocarpa, long dusty rulers of roads ran across the plains. In the late 1930s Canterbury poet D'Arcy Cresswell wrote:

> *The cars here travel very fast, in a great cloud of dust, and with no need of caution; which causes a constant rattle and uproar as the stones, being hurled in the air, strike on their windows and sides. With that travelling dust . . . and the heat and dryness in summer . . . the scene is Arabian almost . . . The plain has everywhere wonderful hues and a pallor and brightness of flame. The gum-trees . . . gleam and shine like the opal of many tints . . . As these disappear, then all at once the mountains are seen, near at hand.*

Beyond the plains, the rough and dusty roads wound into the foothills and mountain uplands, a region that soon became known as the 'high country', inhabited only by sheep-station owners, musterers and their amazing dogs, and occasionally visited by mad mountaineers. The exploits of the runholders, living isolated in the grand and austere landscape beneath the craggy and icy Alps, became the stuff of pioneering legend. One of the most enduring New Zealand myths is of James Mackenzie and his dog, who, in the 1850s, drove a mob of stolen sheep into the high, vast and secret basins of the lake country beneath Mount Cook. Mackenzie as hero symbolises the tough and stoic pioneer man of the high country, but he also represents the colonial as rebel claiming his own piece of land. Mackenzie's collie bitch commands equal fame, representing all those wonderful sheepdogs that made open-range sheep farming possible. The dog monument at Lake Tekapo in the Mackenzie Country attests to the enduring respect and gratitude of their owners.

There are three great roads into the high country. The first, and most spectacular, was built to meet a gold rush when lucky strikes were made on the West Coast in 1864. A Maori greenstone trail from the upper Waimakariri River across the Main Divide was renamed Arthur's Pass after its British rediscoverer. Within a year 1000 men with picks and shovels hacked more than 100 kilometres of coach road from the gorges and riverbeds. Prospectors from all over the world flooded over the 920-metre pass, 500 in one October week of 1865 alone. A Cobb and Co. coach service started in early 1866, taking 36 hours over a journey from Christchurch to Hokitika that

ABOVE: *Great feats of transport engineering have been necessary to overcome the formidable barrier of the Southern Alps between the west and east coasts of the South Island. The latest is a road viaduct above the Otira Gorge, opened in 2000, which bridges mountain country continually subject to earthquake or slip.*

included a dozen river crossings. Little gold was shipped back across Arthur's Pass, but it provided the only transalpine road route for more than 70 years to connect the east and west coasts of the island.

It became a train route also as the railway reached Springfield, at the edge of the plains, in 1880 and was worked through the Waimakariri Gorge country to reach the site of the current Arthur's Pass village in 1914. By then work had been in progress for six years on boring a tunnel under the Main Divide to Otira. A continuous rail route from Christchurch to Greymouth, Hokitika and Westport was finally completed in 1923.

The transalpine route via Arthur's Pass became significant not only as a commercial connection but also as the road to mountain recreation and tourism. The tunnel workers' huts became the basis of an alpine village, winter day trips by train became popular, and skis were first used on the slopes above the pass in 1927. The region became the Mecca for young Canterbury mountaineers who tested their ice axes on Mount Rolleston before moving on to the big peaks further south. In 1929 Arthur's Pass National Park was established, the third in New Zealand.

After the Second World War, diesel railcars ('tin hares') reduced the rail journey time from Christchurch to Arthur's Pass to less than three hours. The West Coast highway was progressively sealed beyond Springfield after 1960, and the improvement of bridges and cuttings culminated in the 2000 opening of a splendid viaduct sweeping down the Otira Gorge. A developing road system brought much of the Canterbury high country within a few hours' drive of Christchurch and stimulated the development of skifields such as Porter Heights and Craigieburn in adjacent subalpine basins. The skiing industry began to boom in the 1960s following the development of the Mount Hutt basin above the Rakaia River, only an hour and half's drive from the city.

The second major highway through the high country and across the Southern Alps was completed in 1937. The route over the Lewis Pass in North Canterbury provides an alternative way to Buller and Nelson, and winds through the most splendid beech forests in the South Island as well as giving rapid access to the thermal district of Hanmer Springs.

The third way to the high country runs from its 'capital' – the country town of Fairlie – and over Burke Pass, not to the West Coast, but to the fabled Mackenzie Country and its icy lakes – Tekapo, Pukaki and Ohau. Through the brown tussocked hills you will spy Aoraki/Mount Cook, a white massif meeting Samuel Butler's 1860 description, 'towering in a massy parallelogram . . . far above all the others . . . no one can mistake it. If a person says he thinks he has seen Mount Cook, you may be quite sure that he has not seen it.' The Mackenzie basin never falls below 300 metres in altitude, stretches for 120 kilometres north to south, and cradles a host of snow-fed rivers that flow together as the great Waitaki ('Weeping Waters'), on which the country's biggest earth dam and hydro-electric system are situated. Dams bar the rivers, new lakes have been formed and old lake levels raised to generate electricity for the power-hungry populations of the east coast and North Island. Pylons like skeletal giants stride over a landscape where aeons ago acres of ice carved away the land for powdery blue lakes and swift grey rivers. The evidence of glacial grinding is still clear – chiselled mountainsides, terraces above the lakes and moraine hillocks beside concrete dams.

Maori made seasonal visits to the Mackenzie lakes to hunt waterfowl, but the land had all been taken up for sheep farming by the mid-1860s. In 1882 the Irish-Swiss team that made the first attempt on Mount Cook could take a train to Fairlie and a coach to Tekapo. But from there the journey was still by horse and wagon over the high downs to Mount Cook station, followed by a perilous crossing of the Tasman River, which regularly consumed horses and drays. The team climbed within 10 metres of the Himalayan-scale summit, but patriots consider that the first real ascent of Cook was made by home-grown Kiwis who spread a sugarbag on the top on Christmas Day 1894.

By that time they could stay (or work) at The Hermitage hotel and there was a rough shingle road from Tekapo to Pukaki ferry and then down the side of the lake to the foot of the great mountain. The Hermitage became the focus of New Zealand's high climbing and mountain tourist industry. All of New Zealand's outstanding guides and amateur climbers have made their

ABOVE: *The biggest earth dam in New Zealand had blocked the Waitaki River by 1965 and created the largest man-made lake – Benmore – with a water capacity one and a half times as great as Wellington Harbour. The dams and lakes of the Mackenzie Country's Upper Waitaki power scheme produce 50 per cent more electricity than all the North Island's hydro stations combined.*

ABOVE: *The Aoraki/Mount Cook massif and Tasman Valley from above Lake Pukaki. Once it required an expedition over rough, flood-prone roads to reach here. Now it is a comfortable four-hour car journey from Christchurch.*

reputations on the thirty 3000-metre peaks within what became known as Mount Cook National Park in 1953 – and celebrated their feats with a drink at The Hermitage bar. Sir Edmund Hillary made his first ascent of Cook in 1947 with top guide Harry Ayres, and went on to complete new climbs with Ayres before venturing to Everest. The scale of the glaciated high peaks of the region made them an ideal training ground for the Himalayas, and New Zealand ice climbers were without peer in the mountains of Nepal and India during the 1950s and 1960s.

Travel to The Hermitage moved progressively from stage coach to open tourer car, to omnibus to plane and private car over roads that were developed into the fastest highways in New Zealand. The challenges of this high mountain landscape also provoked the development of two machines that were to travel the world and reaffirm the skills of Canterbury engineers. On the braided rivers of Irishman Creek station, William Hamilton created the jetboat, capable of navigating the

LEFT: *The top of New Zealand. At 3753 metres, the summit of Aoraki/Mount Cook is the highest point in Australasia. All successful New Zealand climbers in the Himalayas have first flexed their crampons and ice axes on these slopes.*

ABOVE: *Christchurch's River Avon flows through Hagley Park, which was created by the early settlers and named for the country seat of the chairman of the Canterbury Association, Lord Lyttelton.*

shallowest and most fast-running rivers, that went on to storm the Grand Canyon and the Ganges. And at Mount Cook, Harry Wigley perfected a retractable ski-landing system for light planes, and mountain flying techniques that enabled tourists, skiers and climbers to penetrate the most remote corners of the Alps.

Once the Mackenzie Country was synonymous with distance and silence, but now there is no corner that is long free from the sound of engines: of cars, trucks and tourist buses down the black-ribbon highways; of ski-plane, passenger plane and helicopter converging about the nexus of alpine valleys beneath Aoraki/Mount Cook; of jetboats on the lakes, four-wheel-drive vehicles on the riverbeds and farm tracks. The brown and treeless downs and basins have been transformed by plantation, irrigation and chemicals; the rabbit that once devastated this country has been partly controlled with a virus. Cattle have become more profitable than sheep, but the real wealth of the Mackenzie lies in tourism, whether sightseeing through a video camera or adventure tourism in a landscape that offers white and still water, ice, snow and vertiginous rock, fishing, hunting and some of the best gliding skies in the world.

And it no longer takes so long to get there. The train network has shrunk, but the plane from Christchurch to Mount Cook takes just an hour; by car the journey is four hours, the longest it now takes for any road journey from the provincial capital to any part of its large province.

Canterbury is now thoroughly settled and civilized, and Christchurch, with a population of 320,000, has grown to become the South Island's largest city, exceeded in size only by Auckland and Wellington. Its international airport is the base for the biggest Antarctic supply operation in the world, the US military planes of 'Deep Freeze' linking with American and New Zealand bases on the ice throughout the southern summer.

Christchurch and Canterbury have come to conform most closely to the New Zealand provincial pattern based on 'geography, interests and utility', all three more closely bound, developing social distinctions founded not only on historical example but also on a steadier, more even development of society than has occurred in most other parts of New Zealand. There is a merging of identity between town and country that makes Canterbury a state within a state. Canterbury can be seen as the most complete expression of the colonising achievement in New Zealand: planned and orderly, a developed democratic society that has found a balance between the urban and the rural, between agriculture and industry.

ABOVE: *The city of Christchurch from above Sumner and the mouth of the Avon-Heathcote estuary, looking beyond the plains to the foothills of the Southern Alps.*

OTAGO & SOUTHLAND
THE DEEP SOUTH

THE DEEP SOUTH

THE 'DEEP SOUTH' of Otago and Southland is the largest and most distinct region in New Zealand. Its range of grand landscapes – from ocean fiord to scorched Iberian highland to granite island – is without peer. Its climate is more seasonal and more extreme than the rest of the country. Yet more inviting, it seems, to introduced deciduous trees, which flame in frosty inland autumns. This is country for winter fires, long nights and aurora australis, and where spring is a time of renewal and not just a name. This is Murihiku – the Tail End – and while its counterpart Muriwhenua – the North Country – is confidently Pacific, the Deep South seems to have somehow drifted in on the westerlies like a lost chunk of Europe.

At the height of the last ice age, all of Otago and Southland including Stewart Island were covered in ice, fellfields or windswept grasslands, except for coastal strips in the south and east that provided tenuous refuge for relict southern beech and podocarp forest. This provided the seed for the reafforestation of the landscape to the north and west as the ice receded. The seeds of the podocarps, such as rimu, were carried by birds far and wide over all the lowlands of the south. But southern beech forest regenerates only from its edge, like a slowly advancing tide. Over many centuries it colonised the warming grasslands and followed the retreating ice up the river valleys, into the heart of the mountains, over the hard shoulders of Fiordland. But it was too slow for the real incoming tide of sea levels that rose with the ice melt. At last sapling beeches stood helplessly at the edge of a new sea strait that now separated New Zealand's third major island from the coast of the South Island. Stewart Island regenerated its forests without beech, and they came to be dominated by the pale graceful droop of magnificent rimu.

PRECEDING PAGES: *The Upper Hollyford valley and the road to Milford under winter snows.*

LEFT: *Cold winters and hot dry summers have made Central Otago's Clutha Valley famous for its apricots and other stone fruits, such as cherries and peaches. Orchards line the main highway into the western mountains.*

ABOVE: *Mitre Peak and Milford Sound, the apotheosis of Fiordland.*

ABOVE: *The remote Catlins coast of South Otago boasts blowholes, reefs and caves, shipwrecks and good sea fishing.*

The retreating ice also laid bare a geology rare elsewhere. South of the Waitaki Valley – the northern boundary of the region – lies the biggest block of geologically pure country in New Zealand. Almost all of Central and West Otago – south to the Clutha Valley, west to the edge of Fiordland and north to the Alpine Fault – is composed of schist, a rock type found elsewhere only along the narrow band of the highest alps. Butting against this, the Fiordland block is all gneiss and granite; Stewart Island is built of purer granite still. The south-eastern coasts are largely composed of sedimentaries, but Otago Peninsula is volcanic in origin, contemporary with those other once-island volcanoes, Banks Peninsula and the Chatham Islands. There are low-lying alluvial plains and river valleys, especially in Southland, but mostly it is a high and wide country,

embracing the feel of a dry continent's heart in Central Otago and the very image of natural obduracy in the dark, impenetrable tangle of the south-western fiords.

The mountains of Fiordland and the western Alps, rising more than 3000 metres to the summit of Mount Aspiring, garner waterfalls of rain from the prevailing westerlies and cast a vast rain shadow over the rocky mountains and plateaux of 'Central', whose worn aridity is reflected in the name of its mountains – Rock and Pillar, Rough Ridge and the Raggedy Range.

The Deep South claims all the weather extremes. The wettest place in New Zealand is Milford Sound, which averages more than 6500 millimetres of rain a year. The driest place is Alexandra, just 130 kilometres to the south-east, which averages only 350 millimetres a year. The coldest winter temperature ever recorded in New Zealand was minus 21.6°C at Moa Creek in Central Otago. Yet Central regularly registers the summer's top temperature. The Deep South also claims geographical records – it has the South Island's largest (and New Zealand's second largest) lake, Te Anau; its deepest lake, Hauroko; the river with the greatest flow, the Clutha; the country's highest waterfall, the Sutherland Falls (580 metres), and the town farthest from the sea, Cromwell (120 kilometres). The Deep South is indeed New Zealand's 'big country'.

The eastern part of the region found favour with the first Polynesian settlers. The dry valleys and coast were ranged by herds of grazing moa and during the peak of the moa-hunting period, perhaps 600 years ago, these big birds – and the large numbers of seals in coastal colonies – may have supported as many as 8000 people. The extinction of moa, brought about by overhunting, also brought a rapid reduction in the south's human population. Deliberate or accidental fires

ABOVE: *Milford Sound, deep enough to admit an aircraft carrier, too deep for one to anchor. The glaciated slopes of Mitre Peak (left) form the loftiest sea cliffs in the world, 1680 metres high. The Sound is the wettest place in New Zealand, averaging 6500 millimetres of rainfall a year.*

ABOVE: *Impenetrable Fiordland
was the last refuge for both the
flightless moa (Dinornis sp.) and
the so-called 'lost tribe'. Both were
searched for well into the twentieth
century, without success.*

started by the 'moa hunters' also destroyed forests in semi-arid inland areas, which did not regenerate under the rain-shadow conditions of marginal rainfall and extremes of temperature.

The sequence of north–south invasions by successive Maori tribes penetrated even to the Deep South, to the end of the world as they knew it. Waitaha came and were then succeeded by Ngati Mamoe. Ngati Mamoe, it is said, were finally destroyed as a tribe in the seventeenth century by Ngai Tahu in a great battle on the shores of Lake Te Anau. Survivors fled into the wilds of Fiordland, giving rise to the legend of a 'lost tribe' that carried credence well into the twentieth century.

With changing tribes came changing names. New Zealand's third and southernmost island was first known as Te Punga o te Waka a Maui, the anchor stone of Maui's canoe as he fished up the North Island. Later it became Rakiura, 'Glowing sky,' named for both the long sunsets of mid-summer and the flickering of midwinter southern aurora. A northern rendition of this name would be 'Rangiura', and the southern 'k' shows a strong dialectal difference. Similarly, a lake south of Dunedin is named 'Waihola', not the more common northern 'Waihora'. Purists would have it that Rakiura should be spelt 'Lakiula', reflecting the ancient Central Pacific origins of the language. Today, there is even a dialectal difference in English to be found in the Deep South. The 'Southland burr' is the most distinct regional accent in New Zealand English.

Ngai Tahu in Murihiku followed a lifestyle in conformity with the southern seasons. Spring was a time for gathering titi, or muttonbirds – fledgling petrels – from their burrows on nesting islands in Foveaux Strait. The birds were preserved in their own fat inside the bladders of giant kelp seaweed that ribboned the rocky coasts. Kanakana, or lamprey, were caught in their thousands from such prime fishing sites as the falls in the Mataura River. In summer, whanau ranged inland to the great lake country to harvest waterfowl and game birds. And expeditions set out to mine the greenstone in the rivers beyond the head of Wakatipu or, even more adventurously, across the mountains of Fiordland to Milford Sound, Piopiotahi, for the translucent decorative form of the stone named 'takiwai'. In winter the Murihiku people hunkered down in pa on Ruapuke Island, safe from marauding enemies and nurtured by their stores of spring and summer foods.

The last raid by Ngati Toa against Ngai Tahu carried far into the Deep South in 1836. Te Puoho, a relative of Te Rauparaha, led a taua (war party) of about a hundred warriors south from Golden Bay in the longest outflanking movement in the history of Maori warfare. His goal was to surprise and destroy southern Ngai Tahu under the leadership of Tuhawaiki (Bloody Jack), who was based on Ruapuke Island. Te Puoho battled down the length of the West Coast, crossed the Haast Pass and, in traversing the inland lake country and Central Otago, massacred all the inhabitants of isolated villages in case word of his advance reached the Murihiku coast. On the lower Mataura River, Te Puoho's force rushed the settlement of Tuturau and overwhelmed it, but members of a nearby eeling party escaped undetected and took the news to Tuhawaiki. He came

in the night and slaughtered all of the invaders, carrying Te Puoho's head back to Ruapuke in triumph. It was the last Maori battle in the South Island.

Captain Cook first charted Stewart Island as a peninsula, and he tarried in the Deep South only at Dusky Sound during his second voyage in 1773. Nineteen years later the first sealers arrived, following up on Cook's report of 'great numbers' of southern fur seals colonising the reefs and islands. Over the next 30 years the seal population was ravaged along Murihiku's coasts and there was savage interaction between Maori and marauding sealers, the scum of the high seas. Alcohol, tobacco and European diseases were traded by sealers for food and the favours of local women. And when the seal population collapsed, another exploitative industry replaced it – whaling from shore stations established in the 1830s, notably at Aparima (Riverton) in Southland and Otakou at the entrance to Otago Harbour. Isolated farming ventures followed, but extensive European settlement of the Deep South did not begin until 1848, when the Free Church of Scotland settlers arrived to found 'New Edinburgh'. By then disease and demoralisation had reduced the Maori population of Otago and Southland to no more than a few hundred.

The site for the Otago colony encompassed good land, a good harbour, plentiful timber and coal, an invigorating climate, 'all', its surveyor said 'of a character that would attract a humble,

ABOVE: *Some of the 247 original Otago colonists preparing to be ferried down Loch Goil and the Clyde to join the barque* Philip Laing *at the end of 1847. Most would never see their native Scotland again.*

ABOVE: *Dunedin at the start of the gold rushes in 1861. Thirteen years after the first settlers arrived, the struggling town had reached a population of 3000. The rushes increased this sevenfold over the following decade. Reclamation of the harbour foreshore began in the late 1870s. (W. Hatton)*

labouring class of emigrant from their Scottish homeland'. And labour they did, at the heavily bushed country adjacent to their new town of Dunedin. But it was said that the puritan Scots were 'settlers not likely to fail in the hard fight with Nature at the far end of the earth'. Dunedin's first poet John Barr wrote of the struggle:

> *'For either I'm mawin', or thrashin', or sawin',*
> *Or grubbin' the hills wi' the ferns covered fairly.*
> *Grub away, tug away, toil till you're weary,*
> *Haul oot the toot roots and everything near ye.'*

In the first dozen years, the Otago population grew to only 12,000 and scarcely ventured from the coastal margin between Oamaru and Balclutha.

One immigrant who early defied the exhortations of the colony's leaders to keep close to the Dunedin settlement in 'concentration and contiguity' was farmer Nathaniel Chalmers. In September 1853, a month after the government had purchased all Murihiku from surviving Maori, he started from Tuturau with Reko, who had taken part in the killing of Te Puoho's taua, to follow the route of Ngati Toa's 1836 war path. On this incredible journey Chalmers became the first Pakeha to enter the interior of Otago and Southland and to see the great southern lakes of Wakatipu, Wanaka and Hawea. When he could go no further, Reko built a raft from flax stems and piloted him down almost the entire length of the Clutha River to the present day site of Balclutha.

ABOVE: *The Remarkables and
Lake Wakatipu, about 1890. Over
a period of 30 years, Queenstown
went from sheep station to gold-
rush boom town to sleepy hollow.
(E. Smith)*

Chalmers's discovery of the vast and empty tussock lands of Central and Western Otago encouraged speculative pastoralists to establish the first great sheep stations. By the time the official survey of the lakes country between Hawea and Manapouri was begun in 1861 – all one and a half million hectares of it – it was already fully occupied by sheepmen.

The year 1861 was *annus mirabilis* for Otago. In March gold was found below the Lindis Pass. In May there was an even greater find at Gabriels Gully, only 65 kilometres from Dunedin. Waves of men rolled inland from all over New Zealand and Australia, all striving for the richest claim of all. By August 1862 the prospectors had reached the Arrow River and the shores of Wakatipu. Four months later, W. G. Rees's sheep station at the lake had been transformed into the new town of Queenstown, with a population of 4000 diggers.

ABOVE: *Chinese gold miners arrived in Central Otago after the main rush had rolled on and toiled away at small claims, eking out a living over many years. This miner is working a simple sluice box on the banks of the Clutha River in about 1900.*

RIGHT: *High-level dams and water races up to 50 kilometres long were constructed in Central Otago during the later decades of the nineteenth century to provide copious high-pressure water for gold-sluicing operations. Long after the colour of gold has gone, some races still survive and provide irrigation water for farming.*

The tight, close kirk colony of coastal Otago exploded. In two years the province's population jumped from 12,000 to 60,000. And while the first gold rush moved on, to the West Coast in 1864, enormous wealth continued to pour from the goldfields through company mines and dredging operations. Even as late as 1900, 187 huge dredges worked the riverbeds of Central Otago, and the last one did not cease operation until a century after Gabriel Read's find of 'gold like the stars in Orion on a dark, frosty night'.

Gold turned dour little Dunedin into New Zealand's richest city, and Otago into the most populous region, between 1865 and 1900. Dunedin's banks and financial institutions spread the length of the country, bankrolling much North Island farming and commercial development. The city led the country in educational and industrial progress. It established New Zealand's first university – still the southernmost in the world – reflecting strong Scottish traditions of scholarship. The country's first woollen mills opened at Mosgiel in 1872, and the first cargo of frozen meat for England left Port Chalmers in 1882. Gaslight came in 1863, the country's first electric trams in 1900, and New Zealand's finest railway station in 1906. The feeling in Dunedin was neatly contained in Mark Twain's comment when he visited in 1899: 'The people are Scotch. They stopped here on their way from home to heaven – thinking they had arrived.'

Southland's development was slower and more difficult, hindered by the great bogs of the lowland plains and by political wrangling with Otago, which saw it achieve separate provincial status in 1861 and then lose it again in 1870. The city of Invercargill, named for Dunedin's founder, was established in 1856 but 15 years later its population was still only 2000 when Dunedin had passed 20,000. Southland had a more dour and Calvinist reputation than even

Otago, matching what was politely described as a 'rigorous' climate. Prohibition later took good hold, provoking production in the hills near Gore of New Zealand's most famous moonshine whisky, 'Hokonui'. While the early batches were said to be of high quality, later 'paint stripper' brews merited their skull and crossbones labels. Today the Hokonui legend adds much to Gore's reputation as the country music capital of New Zealand.

When the bogs had been drained, the scrub and forest cleared, and fertilisers applied, the Southland plains proved to be the best fat-lamb country in New Zealand. Millions of lambs each year came to be produced for export, and Southland's wealth by the 1960s could be measured by

ABOVE: *By 1900, gold recovery in Central Otago was mostly the business of giant dredges, with few miners turning up at the bank any more to trade gold for cash. In 1901 the last official gold escort guarded the last five bullion boxes on their way to Dunedin.*

FAR LEFT: The upper reaches of the Taieri River, second longest in the South Island, course through the worn and arid rockscapes of the Maniototo and Strath Taieri.

LEFT: New Zealand's third island is Te Punga o te Waka a Maui (Maui's anchor stone), or Rakiura (Glowing sky) or Stewart Island, separated from the South Island by Foveaux Strait. Its soft grey granite landforms, its forests soft with the foliage of rimu and its skies lit by long summer sunsets or winter aurora mark it also as a place separate in character from the rest of New Zealand.

ABOVE: Mason Bay, Stewart Island.

the fact that its citizens paid more per capita in income tax than anywhere else in the country. Although fat-lamb farming has declined during the last couple of decades, Southland now stands on the verge of a new dairying boom.

Lamb exports were shipped out by way of New Zealand's southernmost port, Bluff. This also became famous as the fishing port for Bluff oysters, dredged from the rich beds out towards Stewart Island and tempting the palates of gourmets throughout New Zealand. Auckland restaurants vie to be the first to offer the delicacy at the start of each season in March.

Stewart Island, while administratively part of Southland, has always stood apart across lumpy Foveaux Strait. Maori frequented its environs for muttonbirds and fish, and the sealers and whalers exploited its animals before 1840, but it was not bought for the Crown until 1864. The northern part of the island was logged extensively until 1900, though its rare beech-free forests have regenerated undisturbed for almost a century now. The special quality of Stewart Island's granite and rimu landscapes has been recognised by the recent creation of a national park that covers much of the island's 1750 square kilometres. With a population that has never exceeded several hundred, Stewart Islanders depend for income on tourism and fishing, especially crayfishing and salmon farming. The island was the last refuge of the flightless night parrot, the kakapo. Threatened finally by wild cats, many have been transferred to the predator-free refuge of Whenua Hou (Codfish Island) off the north-west coast, where they have a last chance to survive.

ABOVE: *Most of New Zealand's greatest walking tracks are found in the West Otago-Fiordland region, allowing anyone to experience at first hand the pristine landscapes of south-west New Zealand.*

The western mountain horizons of Otago and Southland long remained a barrier to the tide of settlement and development. The Main Divide of the Southern Alps was breached by hardy gold prospectors, but even the 'discovery' of the easy Maori pass across the mountains (Haast Pass) in 1863 provided a way mainly for hunters and mountain explorers over the following century. All the sounds of Fiordland were accessible only from the sea until the wonders of Milford Sound and the Sutherland Falls led to the discovery of the Milford Track route from Lake Te Anau in 1888. 'The Finest Walk in the World' was the first in a network of great walking tracks that came to be an attraction for all those who wanted to experience at first hand the natural magnificence of the wilds of the Southern Alps and Fiordland. The Routeburn and Hollyford Tracks followed early in the twentieth century, then the Greenstone–Caples, Rees–Dart and, a century after the Milford, the Kepler Track between Lakes Te Anau and Manapouri. Exploration of the high mountain regions and first ascents of the highest peaks were not completed until the 1950s.

After the gold era the 'Southern Lakes' region between Hawea in the north and Manapouri in the south became a favourite destination for Dunedin and Invercargill holidaymakers – and some from further afield – who annually escaped the cool coast for the sun and scenery of the uplands, the fishing and boating. The small lake towns of Wanaka, Queenstown and Te Anau catered for these Christmas visitors as well as being service centres for their pastoral farming communities. It took time to reach them, over long dusty roads, winding through the apricot and peach

orchards of Central, on through the deep Cromwell and Kawarau Gorges to the glacial blue glare of Wakatipu or Wanaka. As Otago poet James K. Baxter declared:

Upon the upland road

Ride easy, stranger

Surrender to the sky

Your heart of anger.

The sun-drenched stillness of Central reflected a certain somnolence that had settled over all Otago after the First World War as the centres of industry, business and population shifted inexorably to the North Island's Auckland and Wellington. But while Dunedin and the coastal regions languished, inland Otago began to go through changes in the 1950s that would transform the region over the following 40 years. In 1952 New Zealand's largest national park, Fiordland, was established and the development of visitor facilities began. Two years later the opening of the Homer Tunnel completed road access to Milford Sound from Te Anau. The Lindis Pass road from Mount Cook and the Mackenzie Country was upgraded, so that when the Haast Pass road to the West Coast was opened in 1965 – through the newly created Mount Aspiring National Park – a network of top tourist motoring routes had been completed.

In 1960 a commercial skifield was opened at Coronet Peak, near Queenstown, the beginning of a ski industry that has since spread the length of the Southern Alps and includes the more recent Remarkables field and two near Wanaka. Airfields were developed at Queenstown and Wanaka; roads were progressively widened and sealed, partly as a consequence of the changes to the landscape wrought by the major hydro-electric power schemes on the Clutha River at Roxburgh (1962) and Clyde (1995). The country's biggest power station, underground at the head of Lake Manapouri (1970), was constructed to provide power for New Zealand's only aluminium smelter, near Bluff.

By the 1990s Queenstown, Wanaka and Arrowtown were only four hours' driving time from Dunedin. All had become favourite weekend destinations, whether for summer watersports or winter skiing. Trunk airline connections with northern centres brought inland Otago skiing within reach of all New Zealanders. In the 1990s direct flights between Queenstown and Sydney

ABOVE: *Mountain bikers on the Remarkables skifield road during a stage of the Southern Traverse endurance race. Over the last 20 years, the Otago lakes district and mountains have become the most popular venue for adventure sports and tourism activities based in the resort of Queenstown.*

RIGHT: *Attracting prospectors in the late 1860s gold rush, Macetown, on the Arrow River, was a thriving settlement with a population of about 3000 at its peak. However, within 50 years the prosperous town declined and all but disappeared. Now little more than the remaining exotic trees and a stone cairn mark the place where Macetown once flourished.*

meant that New Zealand skiing was within a few hours' travel for Australians. From the 1980s a new kind of tourism was developed, with Queenstown as its base. 'Adventure tourism' came to mean not only high climbing, heliskiing and mountain biking, but also white-water rafting and canoeing, high-speed jetboating, paragliding, 'fly by wire' and, above all, bungy jumping, which was first launched from the area's high canyon bridges. Since 1990 Queenstown has left behind its old image of a sleepy family holiday town and has grown almost exponentially to city size. The hottest resort in New Zealand – hundreds of thousands of tourists fly and motor in from all over the world – it has recently become a favoured location for international movies.

The heritage of the legendary gold-rush era underpins the tourist attraction of the Queenstown–Arrowtown area. The spectacle of old poplar and willow trees colouring the rugged landscape in autumn recalls the first tough pioneers who began to make something of this empty and harsh country 140 years ago. Goldfields heritage in the shape of ruined stone cottages, old pubs, abandoned mine sites and the sluiced-out Blue Lake of St Bathans in Central Otago lend an historical human texture to a landscape already worn old by wind and sun. Parts of Central are now also being transformed from overgrazed or rabbit-worn sheep runs into vineyards, new orchards and olive groves in a horticultural revolution that

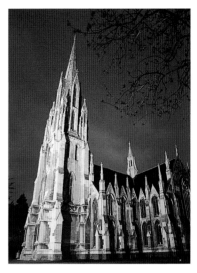

Above: *First Church is the most elegant example of Dunedin's 19th century architectural heritage.*

promises to turn the South Island's heartland into a southern Iberia.

Heritage – human and natural – and education now form the core of Dunedin's character and wealth. The city is the only genuine 'university town' in New Zealand, its economic activity dominated by the booming University of Otago, with associated medical schools and neighbouring educational institutions. Dunedin's educational heritage is reflected in old stone college buildings that date back to the 1860s. A larger architectural heritage, both civic and domestic, has survived from the city's Victorian and Edwardian heyday, lending Dunedin a patina of age, of permanence found nowhere else in New Zealand, except for the 'whitestone' Victorian-era precinct of North Otago's Oamaru.

Dunedin is also home to the world's third-largest natural history film-making unit, drawing for much of its material on the variety of unspoiled land and sea environments of southern New Zealand. As if recognising its links to the natural world, Dunedin city's boundaries range far into the dry hills of Central Otago and encompass the Otago Peninsula. Taiaroa Head, at the extremity of the peninsula, is the only mainland breeding ground for the royal albatross. Yellow-eyed penguins nest in its open sea bays, and both fur seals and Hooker's sea lions grace its beaches. Within a short span, Dunedin encapsulates the unmatched cultural and natural heritage of the Deep South.

INDEX

S. Pacific Ocean

West Coast

Southern Alps.

Mt Cook 13,200.

L. Tekapo.

 kaki

ring
rt

· Scotchman's Hut

Mountains Real.

Burke's Pass
Fire against Fire
Hard Lines
Mt Exhaustion
Alford F.
20,00

No personal reflections.
A Starlight Camp

Ghosts of legs of Mutton
Fire & a Chop
Dog's leg & Lobster Salad

R. Opihi

Old French

Look Out

Cold Bishop

Opuwa R.
Opuha R.
Winter Nights, no roof

Hoa

Half & Half
Lost in the Opihi
Wet to the Saddle
Journeys with Sheep

Arrowenua
Ninety Mile Be

R. Orari
R. Rangitata
R. Hinds
R. Harketer

The

R. Arrowenua

Timaru.
S. Pacific Oce

R. Waihao

Chart of the present Province of Canterbury, New Zealand, as rough
Mount Cook Range is crossed by about 1